# Me, Myself & I

## *My Life So Far*

A MEMOIR BY

## *Dorothy S. Litwin*

**M** Mosaic Design
Book Publishers

# Me, Myself & I
## My Life So Far

First Printing – October 2016

ISBN: 978-0-9968933-3-6 *(paperback)*

Printed in the United States of America on acid-free paper.

Published by Mosaic Design Book Publishers
Dearborn, Michigan USA

0  1  2  3  4  5  6  7  8  9

# ACKNOWLEDGEMENTS

I could not have written this book without help from my four sons, particularly Jim, who started the whole process by interviewing me on camera for two straight days and then transcribing every word.

I also want to thank Susan Giffin for her editing work.

# PREFACE

This Robert Frost poem sums up my life:

> Two roads diverged into a wood, and
> I took the one less traveled by and
> That has made all the difference.

I always seemed to follow my own direction—not dating, not going away to college and living on campus, never acting "boy crazy," and not being interested in make-up, fashion or "girly" things. My aunt Carrie thought there was something wrong with me! I loved reading, and everyone knew to give me books for my birthdays. I loved classical music, going to the movies alone, and generally, I was "different."

When Frank Sinatra sang "My Way," I felt he was singing about me. In my life, I had many choices, and I really "did it my way."

Now I am ninety years old. I can hardly believe it! When we're young, time seems to move so slowly, but as we age, time just flies by. I don't know how I could be ninety; it's incredible. Where did the time go?

I have clear memories of my very early childhood, probably when I was four or five years old. Now I can't remember what I did yesterday. But here I am.

One comment on the title of this book: In high school when I was sixteen, we had an assignment to write our autobiography. My father liked what I wrote so much that he arranged with his printer employer to have the pages mounted and bound as a book. In researching my new book, I found my old book buried in a box. That inspired this title, as I am simply "filling-in" the seventy-four years that have passed since I wrote the original!

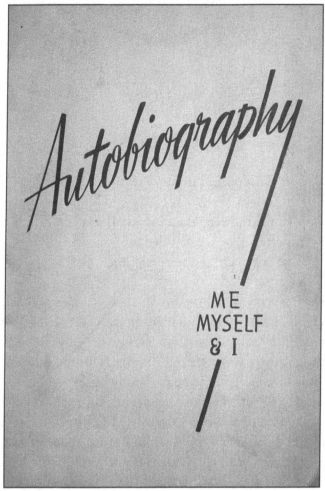

*The original Me, Myself & I book*

Many times during my ninety years, people have said to me, "You should write a book because of the unusual or not so everyday experiences you've had." Therefore, I decided to do it. I don't know if anyone cares to read it, but here goes...

Dorothy Litwin
September 2016
Huntley, Illinois

# CONTENTS

# My Mother's Family
## 1882 and On

My maternal grandparents, Nettie and Max Schwartz, came to the United States from Hungary. My grandfather was seventeen when he came in 1882 and first went to Denver to settle down as he had some distant Schwartz relatives living there. I wish he'd stayed there. I would have loved growing up in Colorado instead of Illinois. I remember him describing Denver as very clean, and when it rained and after the sun came out, the streets would be so clean that they sparkled and were just beautiful.

When he was twenty-eight, he heard about the 1893 World's Fair in Chicago and wanted to see it. He got on a train, went to Chicago, and settled down there, and that's where he met my grandmother, Nettie (Moya) Ackerman, who was living in the same boarding house. People stayed

*Moya*

in boarding houses in those days, not hotels. I'm not sure that they even had hotels then. Nettie was a very beautiful woman and had a lovely singing voice. The story goes that she had an offer to go on the stage as a singer. But in those days, people thought the stage was not a nice place for a young woman.

After they got married, they opened a cleaning and tailoring shop in the Wicker Park neighborhood and later in Logan Square. They both were excellent tailors, and they sent the cleaning out to a professional cleaning company. Their store in Logan Square was on the northeast corner of Spaulding and Wellington, and they lived in a one-bedroom apartment at the back of the store. On the other three corners, there was a tavern, a grocery store, and a candy shop.

They had three children: my uncle Joe the oldest; my aunt Carrie in the middle; and my mother Bertha, called Bertie, the baby. They all graduated from Lakeview High School. Uncle Joe married Sarah and they had three sons: Dick, the oldest; Ed in the middle; and Bob, the youngest. Dick and Bob have passed on, but Ed and I are both ninety and still here.

Aunt Carrie married Harry, a very talented designer of custom jewelry, and he became very wealthy. One of his regular clients was the Goldblatt family, owner of Chicago's many famous department stores. They had three children: Sally, the oldest; Jack, the middle one; and Ronnie, the baby. Carrie and Harry lived in a large, beautifully furnished apartment around the corner from my grandparents' store.

We also lived one block away from the tailor store, so we were all in the same neighborhood, and my cousins Sally and Jackie, my sister Laverne, and I all grew up together.

We spent a lot of time at Grandma and Grandpa's store. Grandmother Nettie was a wonderful baker and cook. The story about her nickname Moya is that when Dick was learning to talk, he couldn't pronounce "grandma." It came out sounding like "Moya." Whether that is fact or fiction, I don't know, but even though her name was Nettie, everyone from family, friends and the whole neighborhood began calling her Moya and that name stuck.

My maternal grandfather, Max, was eighty when he died in 1945, and after my grandmother died in 1937, he must have sold the store

*My grandfather Max*

and moved in with us in our apartment at Sunnyside and Kedzie.

Max was a short man with a big knobbly growth on the back of his head. I don't know what it was, but it fascinated me. It was always there, but it didn't seem to bother him at all. He was a small man with a big temper. He had no trouble telling off people. Moya was a sweet, wonderful woman whom everybody loved; that was why the customers always came to her.

*My grandma Moya: On one side is my dad, Mert, and on the other side is Uncle Joe. Could that be our place on Spaulding and Barry?*

My grandfather and my dad used to fight when they played cards. I don't remember much more about Max. But I do remember that when my Moya died, my uncle Joe was in the room where she just had passed away. He was completely broken up. I remember trying to comfort him, but he gently shoved me away. It was something I never forgot. In every family, there's usually one person that people go to for problem solving, and that was Uncle Joe. Everyone depended on him. I think in our immediate family, my Al was the one everyone consulted.

# My Father's Family
## 1877 and On

My father's parents were born in Lithuania, came to this country when they were young, and met in Chicago. My grandfather Robert Sapero was born in 1877 came to Chicago in 1894. My grandmother Jennie Ziv, was born in 1880 and arrived here when she was eighteen. They met and married in Chicago.

The Ziv family name was big in the early motion picture business. My paternal grandfather Robert actually owned a Nickelodeon, which was a little movie theater that showed silent movies and cost only a nickel to enter; hence the name. I don't know how long he had it or what he did with it, and I don't remember ever going

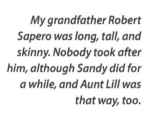

*My grandfather Robert Sapero was long, tall, and skinny. Nobody took after him, although Sandy did for a while, and Aunt Lill was that way, too.*

there. (The only Nickelodeon I ever went into was the one at the Museum of Science and Industry. I used to love taking my boys there). Grandfather Robert got a job working for AT&T. I think he might have been a janitor. I think it was not a big job, but that's where he worked until he retired.

My grandmother Jennie didn't work at all. She and my grandfather had four children; my father Merton was the eldest. My aunt Ethel was the second, my aunt Lil was the third in line, and my aunt Miriam was the baby. Aunt Miriam married Hyman Ross, and they had two children, my cousins Barbara and Bill. My aunt Lil married Hy's brother, Oscar Ross. The two weddings were almost a month apart. Lil and Oscar adopted Joan, and then they had a baby of their own, Ellyn.

My dad's other sister, Ethel, married Charles Jacobs. He was a "bookie," which meant that he placed bets on horse races and became quite wealthy. They never had a child of their own but adopted a baby boy and named him Harris. When Charles died, Ethel married a great man named Joe Castle who was in the wholesale poultry business. Many years later, Laverne's husband, Maury Roth, actually worked for his company.

My paternal grandfather's name was Robert Sapero. As the story goes, when an immigration agent asked his name, he heard it as SAPERO, but it probably should have been SHAPIRO, although I'm only guessing.

I wasn't particularly close with that part of the family. I guess it's true; children are usually closest to their mother's side of the family. I don't know why that is.

# Aunts, Uncles & Cousins

Aunt Carrie was my mother's older sister, Caroline Goldstein. When I was very young, I remember that she was married to Harry Goldstein. We were all very close; we used to see each other almost every day. Aunt Carrie and Uncle Harry had a large apartment on Dawson Avenue, one block from Moya and two blocks from me. He

*This is Dick and Ed, the two brothers Schwartz. Dick died of cancer. The last time I saw him, Al and I were in Las Vegas. He was there with his family at the same hotel, and we bumped into each other. It was such a surprise.*

*This is Uncle Joe and a friend in one of those photo booths where they had their picture taken in a fake car.*

was a jewelry designer and made a lot of money. They had a live-in maid, Betty. Sally, Jackie, Laverne, and I spent a lot of time at their house when we weren't with Moya. Monopoly was a very new and an extremely popular board game, and we would play for hours on the dining room table.

*This is a picture of my cousin Bob Schwartz, Uncle Joe, and his mother Sarah.*

*My mother was sitting on this thing in front of the building, I think on Dawson Avenue where Uncle Harry and Aunt Carrie had an apartment. We kids played Buck Rogers and that was like our rocket ship.*

*This is Aunt Sarah, my mother, and Aunt Carrie. In the background are Uncle Joe and my dad.*

Growing up in the depression years, my father was sometimes out of work. He was a printing salesman. When I was in eighth grade, he got a new and very good job, and we did pretty well for a while. We even had a new car, a Buick, his favorite car, and he treasured it. Only Dad drove it, but then not many women were driving cars anyway. When we had no car, we had to walk, take buses, L-trains, and streetcars to get anywhere we wanted to go. We didn't think about it; that was the way it was.

Aunt Carrie and Uncle Harry got divorced when I was about eleven. Divorce back then was rare and somewhat shameful. He left Carrie, pregnant with Ronnie, and their two young children, Sally and Jackie, and never gave her any financial support. She had to leave their beautiful home and go to work. One of her jobs was working in a school cafeteria where she washed dishes and did other menial jobs. Meanwhile, Uncle Harry remarried and started a new family. With no financial support from Harry, Carrie became destitute and had no place to live. My father was out of work again, and we all—my dad, my mom, Laverne, and I—got together with Aunt Carrie, Sally, Jackie, and baby Ronnie and rented a bungalow at 4442 N. Francisco Avenue in a very nice Chicago neighborhood called Ravenswood Manor.

My mother's brother Joe (Uncle Joe) and his family lived in the

Edgewater neighborhood of Chicago. We didn't see much of them, but they usually came to visit Moya on the weekends, and they would occasionally invite us over for dinner, which was a big, big deal because they had a huge, beautiful apartment.

Uncle Joe worked for an insurance company and later, after he left the army, he started his own insurance company. The office was located in the Insurance Exchange Building at 175 West Jackson Blvd. It became a very, very big, successful agency, and it still is.

*Laverne and Jackie as little kids with Aunt Carrie in the background*

His sons Ed and Bob joined the firm, but Dick, the oldest, did not want to go into the insurance business. He was a musician, and when he was drafted, he played French horn in the Fifth Army Band. He served in Europe in WWII, and during the war, he sustained an injury in a plane crash that affected his mouth. After that, he was no longer able to play the French horn, so he began playing the accordion. After he left the army, he played with the Grant Park Symphony and taught

*This is a picture of Uncle Joe in the army during World War I where he served in Europe. I believe he was in combat, but when he came back, he never talked about that time.*

accordion at 1 Wabash Avenue in downtown Chicago. Later, he and his wife, Jean, moved to Wausau, Wisconsin, where he opened a music school, and taught the accordion and other instruments. Later, they moved to Florida where he opened another music school.

My aunt Sarah was one of five girls born in Kiev, Russia. She was a wonderful cook but was always dieting. When Al and I moved into our first house on Wilson Avenue, she introduced me to one of her friends who had a beautiful mid-size grand piano for sale. Our house had a huge living room, so we bought it, and I still have that piano today. She also gave me her KitchenAid mixer, which I still have, and she did many other things to help me.

*This picture is of Uncle Joe standing in front of the Spaulding and Barry apartment building where we lived.*

# *My Parents*

My mother's name was Bertha Schwartz Sapero, but everybody called her Bertie. She always loved the name Blossom and might have changed it officially, but in those days, people didn't change their names, so it was always Bertie. We were very, very close, and I miss her to this day. She and my father were both born in 1900—my mother on October 27 and my father on November 6—so I guess she was a couple of weeks older than he was. That was the butt of a couple of jokes between them. My mother and father got married on New Year's Eve. We always could remember their anniversary date.

*Mom and Dad's wedding*

*This is July 1923, a group of women with my mother, second from the right, but I don't remember who the others are.*

My mom was very beautiful, had a lovely singing voice like Moya, and joined choirs whenever she could. She loved fun—clothes, makeup, parties, dancing. Unfortunately, when the Depression hit, things were tough for both of them. We had to move a lot, didn't always own a

*Another photo of my mother with people I don't know.*

car, and at one time had to split up and live with other relatives. She had to work part-time as a sales girl when things were difficult. She loved to talk to people and had many friends.

My mother got a job at a millinery store in Logan Square. The word millinery is a word you hardly hear any more. A millinery store was one that sold women's hats. When I was young, all women wore hats; men also wore hats called fedoras. Both of these types of stores

*My mother was a flirt. She loved parties, dancing, and clothes.*
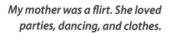

are no longer around. My mother loved working there and was very good at sales.

I had a younger sister, Laverne Jacqueline. (I never decided how to spell her name. Was it LaVerne, LaVergne or Laverne?) She was born on November 6, 1927, and she was two years younger than I. Growing up, we shared a double bed. I liked to read in bed before falling asleep, and we had many a fight about keeping the light on so I could read. My father always came in to break up the fight, and he always spanked Laverne instead of me. I don't know why, but it always stopped the fight.

Laverne, my dad, and I used to wait for my mother until she finished work at night. We'd walk over to Milwaukee Avenue where her store was located and then all walk home together. We always passed the same delicatessen; I remember that so clearly. It had the most delicious potato salad, something I don't eat anymore. We'd pick up some cold cuts and, of course, the potato salad and rye bread, and that would be our supper.

My mother never drove a car, and after my father passed away in 1959, she, of course, owned his Buick. My Al taught her to drive, and she got a driver's license when she was sixty. That took a lot of nerve. She got a job at Joseph's Shoe store in the Old Orchard shopping center and drove my dad's beloved Buick to work every day.

One day, when she was coming home from work, she wanted to make a left turn into Keeler Avenue where we lived. Someone hit her car in the rear. She wasn't injured, but she stopped driving after that.

My mother was always very healthy, but one day her doctor detected a heart murmur. He guessed she might have had measles or the mumps as a child, which probably affected a heart valve. He recommended a "minor" surgical procedure, so she decided to have it done at Edgewater Hospital. Laverne and I stayed in the waiting room during the procedure. After a while, we decided we needed some fresh air and left the hospital to take a walk outdoors. When we returned, the doctors berated us. They had discovered that Mother had breast cancer, and they wanted to do a mastectomy. They had come down to the waiting room to get our permission to perform the surgery. We weren't there, and, although they went ahead with the mastectomy and cancelled the valve replacement originally scheduled, they sternly

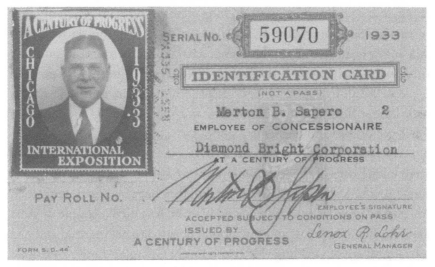

*Dad's World's Fair ID*

warned, "Never, never leave the hospital during a family member's surgery." From that moment on, we never did.

Another time, my mother began having odd things happen to her. Wherever she was, she would fall asleep, and the doctors couldn't figure out what was wrong. While looking through *Time* magazine one day, I read an article about people with her symptoms, and their diagnosis was myasthenia gravis. I immediately told her doctor, and he said, "I was about to tell you what she has." Face-saving, I guess. Anyway, she began treatment and eventually recovered. The Greek shipping magnate Ari Onassis had it, but he never recovered from it.

What else can I tell you about that era? The World's Fair was in Chicago for two years starting in 1933, and I remember we went there once when I was about eight or nine. I have a picture of my father when he was working there. I was so young, and all I remember was seeing many flags of different countries. That's it. I was too young really to appreciate its significance.

My dad wasn't close with us at all. We could never could sit down and talk to him about issues, but my mother and I were very close. She would be washing dishes and I would be drying them, and we would be singing and harmonizing. That was the most fun. She had a beautiful singing voice and used to belong to choirs. I did the same thing, and now Jim does it. And Doug seems to have inherited my love of music. Starting in fifth grade, he learned to play the clarinet. He's still playing it, as well as the piano, saxophone, percussion, and any other wind instrument—that's about sixty years of music. It's genetic, I guess. We all had great voices. I kept joining choirs until a few years ago. I went from alto to second alto and most recently to tenor. My voice got deeper and deeper as I got older.

My father died in 1959 while living in our Skokie house. They were taking care of the kids while we were still in the hospital. I don't remember how she met Al Rosenfeld, but they began going out together. He had two married daughters, and his wife had died a couple of years earlier. After a while, Al and my mother decided to get married and had a beautiful small wedding. He had a lovely Georgian house in Rogers Park, and she moved there after their wedding.

She loved the idea of living in that house, having lived in apartments her whole life. My kids thought it was fun to visit because in their basement, he had a built-in bar and a slot machine. The boys used the machine until I think he stopped them. He was extremely possessive about his things.

One time, my mother bought a wall clock and wanted to hang it on a wall in the kitchen. I said, "I can do that for you." I was on the ladder, trying to hang it up, but he came in and wouldn't let me do it; after all, this was where he and his wife had lived, and he didn't want anything changed. His two married daughters really seemed to resent the fact that he had remarried. But my mom and Al Rosenfeld seemed very happy. Once diagnosed with prostate cancer, after a very short time, he passed away.

I guess his daughters sold the house, so my mom moved to Skokie with Al and me. She decided she wanted a condo in a brand new development that had been built along the Chicago River. She applied and eventually purchased one. The buildings were Winston Towers 1, 2 and 3. She loved it there, and she worked over at the JCC (Jewish Community Center) in the gift shop, which she adored. That was her thing; she loved waiting on people. She and I spent happy days furnishing the place, and so she began a new chapter in her life.

I was heavily involved with the Centre East theatre at the time, and one night I received two free tickets to the theater in Golf Mill. I drove my mother and her friend to the theater. Laverne and her husband Maury were away on a trip, so they weren't available to pick them up and take them home, and I had a meeting at Centre East that night.

When I returned home after my meeting, I called Mom, and there was no answer. After several tries and still no answer, I called one of her friends who lived down the hall from her and asked her to knock on my mother's door to see if she was all right. She called me back to tell me there was no answer, so I got in my car and drove over there.

I had a key, so I opened the door. I found her dead on her bathroom floor. She must have been on the toilet and fell down from there because her pants were down. I remember trying to cover her while I called 911. I was in total shock. The phone rang and I picked it up. It was Laverne calling from California, just to say hello. I told her what had just happened, and she broke down and said she was coming home.

My mom's neighbors were now in the house, trying to help me. The EMTs came and eventually took her away. I don't remember much after that, except the next day I found myself in a grocery store; I don't know why, just walking around.

There was a funeral and a burial after that, of course, but I don't remember much of that, either. My mother was my best friend. We'd talk at least once a day, every day. I missed her so much. Al was a great comfort to me; he took care of all the arrangements. I guess he sold the condo, her car, and everything else.

# My Sister Laverne

My sister was not a reader nor did she share an interest in things I enjoyed; later on, we became very close. In fact, just the other day, I almost picked up the phone to tell her something and then realized that she has been gone for years. She was a good student but not a great student; she didn't care about school that much, although I loved it.

Laverne loved to dress up. She was just like my mother that way. They both loved clothes and makeup. As long as my clothes were clean, it didn't matter to me what I wore. Laverne and I went to Roosevelt High School and graduated there. So did our cousins Jack and Sally. Carrie had a younger child named Ronnie who also attended Roosevelt.

Laverne married Maury Roth when she was eighteen. The wedding was in our apartment on Sunnyside Avenue. They had three children: Norman followed by

*Laverne and me on Hollywood Avenue; yes, she's riding a tricycle.*

*I think that's Laverne and me. People would come around the neighborhood with a pony and take pictures of the kids.*

*Laverne, Mom, and me*

Susan, and then Nancy.

Maury's parents Rosie and Sam had a grocery store, and they knew my grandparents. They had two sons, Maury and Sid. They all met somewhere, and that's how Laverne met Maury. Laverne was

*Here's Laverne and me in the Fred Fox Studio. We knew the Fred Fox people because we all belonged to the same temple. I hated this picture because he would puff out our dresses, making us look very fat. The hair was funny too, very strange.*

*That's my cousin Ed with Laverne in the middle and me on the other side. My grandma Moya is behind us. We were in front of the apartment building on Spaulding and Barry where we lived on the third floor. We were in an L, the part that juts out. It's funny how one remembers those things.*

*That's Laverne and Maury. They were dating at that point probably.*

eighteen when they got married. But she was happy being married.

Maury worked in wholesale meat sales, and their first house was on Hull Street in Skokie. That house was just north of the train tracks. The Illinois Central commuter trains used those tracks, but the Skokie Swift eventually replaced them. The house was also across the street from a huge CTA (Chicago Transit Authority) yard for buses and trains. Our kids played softball on the empty lot, and their backyard was famous for Maury's famous barbecued chicken, which he always cooked until it turned black. They had a dog named Sparky. One feature of the house was that they could see the screen of the drive-in theater, and although the picture was very small, the kids thought it was very cool. Later, they moved further north in Skokie to Grosse Point Road, a few of blocks from my house, also in Skokie. Our children were very close, and they always played together. Most of them graduated from Highland grammar school and Niles North High School.

Laverne and I were very, very good friends, and we helped each other always, whether it was babysitting, shopping or just getting together. Laverne was still smoking, and I had just quit. I was a heavy smoker, having started in my TV days when everybody smoked. One day, we were outside watching the kids playing. Suddenly, one of the kids started to run into the street to get a ball, and Laverne saw that, handed her lit cigarette to me, and went after the kid. Old habits die slowly, and I was remembering that movie, *Dr. Strangelove*. I had all I could do not to put it in my mouth. Like Dr. Strangelove, I used my other hand to grab the cigarette and knock it away. But, you know, the urge was still there. Not anymore. Today I couldn't care less about smoking. There is a home movie of me stirring a pot of chili, with my right hand while my left hand held a cigarette. As the story goes, I dropped ashes in the chili. I'm not sure that happened.

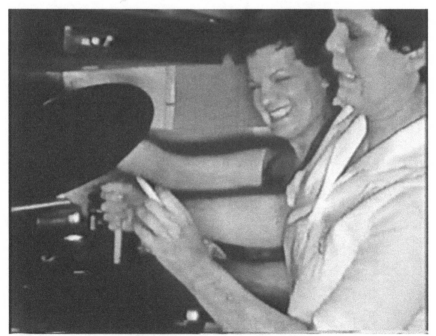

*This is a still of a home movie showing me stirring a pot of chili with my mother.*

# My Early Childhood

I began in Chicago. I was born on October 14, 1925, and my parents were Merton (Mert) Benjamin Sapero and Bertha (Bertie) Schwartz Sapero.

*My mom and dad on the beach; they used to spend a lot of time in the dunes in Indiana.*

That's me posed in a picture that my mother thought was so cute; she sent it to the newspaper for a baby contest. They used to have baby contests years ago. They should do things like that again. People reach back to things that happened fifty or sixty years ago. They were good ideas then, and they would be good ideas now.

This is my grandma Moya holding me. What a bonnet that was! She was wonderful. She had very long hair and always wore it in a bun. And all the women at that time wore housedresses. They were made of cotton, usually in the South. My grandma used to make her own, very simple, and that's what women wore around the house. No women wore slacks. It would have been unthinkable in those days.

A while back, I was having an MRI. I know that the drum-like sound and the enclosed cylinder can drive many people up the wall, but for some reason, I found myself almost hypnotized by the sound, and I began remembering things that happened when I was about four or five years old. I was in the apartment on Hollywood Avenue in Chicago. I knew the entire layout of the place, where my sister and I had slept, and the location of the kitchen, living room, and back entrance, and even the fact that we were on the first floor of a yellow brick building. It was so real that when the technician said, "You're all done," I said, "Oh, no! I was having such an interesting time." Was I dreaming, hypnotized or?

My earliest memory is living in that yellow brick building, and I even remember the address, 1518 Hollywood Avenue. It was in Chicago just east of Clark Street near Ashland Avenue in the Edgewater neighborhood. I started kindergarten at Pierce School from that apartment, and there was a small park a block away on Clark Street where we played. My mother's brother Joe (Uncle Joe), Aunt Sarah, and their three boys lived nearby.

We kids were in awe of them because they had a big, beautiful apartment, and my cousins went to "go-away" camp. I remember all those things, even though I was very young, probably five years old.

I spent so much time with Moya that I clearly remember the layout of her "back of the store" apartment. In particular, I remember her kitchen. There was a hand-cranked coffee grinder on the wall. There was also a pantry—every apartment had a pantry, which was a small room in the kitchen. There was a refrigerator in the pantry, a white metal table, chairs, and a gas stove.

My grandmother made wonderful main dishes and delicious baked goods—strudel, pogacsa (quick Hungarian biscuits), and other great pastries. She used to make strudel on that kitchen table, and when the dough was ready, she would stretch it so that it hung over the table edges like a tablecloth. She would cover it with melted butter, sugar, cinnamon, nuts, and sometimes raisins or apples, roll it into a long roll, and bake it. Wow, was it delicious. She also had wonderful Hungarian main dishes. We ate chicken paprikash, stuffed cabbage, goulash, and cabbage fried with noodles. Of course, everything milchedich (dairy in Yiddish) was made with tons of butter. BUTTER MAKES ANYTHING TASTE WONDERFUL! Besides the butter, let's not forget sour cream. The word "diet" was unknown. We ate butter, put sour cream on everything, and just enjoyed ourselves. I guess there was margarine, but in those days, I never heard or saw it. Later I experienced it for the first time. Margarine was white in those days. Later, we could add yellow food coloring to make it more palatable. Just to illustrate how unknown it was, it was banned in Wisconsin and other dairy states.

Next to the kitchen was a combination dining room/living room. It had a floor model radio, chairs, and a buffet. My grandmother listened to her favorite soap operas every day, and I got familiar with *My Gal Sunday* and other "soaps" while my grandfather listened only to the news. Moya also worked in the store, waiting on customers, doing clothing repairs, and helping my grandfather. Everybody loved her.

I remember there were two ways to get into their store/apartment. It was a semi-basement, and to get into the store, there was a door

*This picture shows me in 2012 at that building after at least seventy-five years. The darker bricks I am pointing to are where the original entrance to the store had been bricked-over.*

on the Spaulding side. When you opened that door, there were about four stairs to take down into the store. Those kinds of apartments were known as English basements.

To go into the apartment itself, we could enter through the store or enter through the building's main lobby, ring their doorbell, and when they "buzzed" us in, we would enter another small lobby. Then we would open the door with our key, enter the apartment, go down four more steps, and we were there. The door leading into the store was across from those steps on the right, but the bathroom was directly across from the steps. Turning left, we would pass the one bedroom, continue on to a combination living/dining room, and then enter the kitchen.

In the store, under the Spaulding street windows there was a large Singer sewing machine with a big foot pedal, all operated manually; no such thing as an electric sewing machine. Stepping on the foot pedal provided the power to operate the machine. Across the back of the store was a counter, and to its side a large glass case where they placed finished clothing. My cousin, Ed, told me that when they made their usual Sunday visits, he and his brothers would hide in the store's glass case among all the clothes hanging there. The only problem, he said, was that nobody was looking for them.

Under the Wellington side window was a big table on which there was an ironing board that my grandfather called his "biggle" board. On the board, he kept this big wooden block. When he ironed something, he would spray water on the item, would put a cloth over it, smack this block of wood down, and then press the iron over it, creating a cloud of steam. I guess that was an early version of a steam iron. My sister Laverne and used to hang out there a lot, watching him while our parents were working. It was around the corner from my school, so we had our own little insular island with family right there beside us all the time.

I spent many times in that basement store and the apartment behind it. I remember one Fourth of July, people were shooting off firecrackers all around the building area, and it scared me so much that I climbed under my grandmother's bed and stayed there until they stopped.

*This interesting picture is all of us cousins—Sally, Jackie, Laverne, and me, but not Ronnie, as I think he had not been born yet. Just posing but it looks like it might have been in front of my grandparent's store, the corner tailor shop. I remember those windows on the side.*

During the Depression, my father lost his job again. We had no car (he loved all Buicks), so we moved in with my paternal grandparents in the Wicker Park neighborhood. My sister contracted scarlet fever while living there. She was very sick, and my mother moved into their room with her. The Chicago Health Department placed them on quarantine, as required by law. They posted a big red sign on their bedroom door, warning everyone not to enter. They had to stay there, and no one could enter. My mother and sister were locked in that bedroom for a couple of weeks, and I wasn't allowed to see them, only talk through the door. We used to put the food outside their door; they couldn't leave that room except to go to the bathroom. It was a very lonely time for all of us.

One night, my father took me to see a scary movie featuring Lon Chaney. I don't remember the title, but it was the hot film at the time. It scared the heck out of me. That night when we got back to the house, my father, who was a big cigarette smoker, said, "Oh, I forgot to

*My mother, father, and I are on the rocks at Montrose Harbor; we used to spend a lot of time there. We liked it a lot.*

buy cigarettes. I'll be right back." So, he left me alone in this giant apartment, and after just seeing that film, I was terrified being alone. My grandparents and aunts were already asleep, and I was by myself. I still remember that. I must have been about six years old, I guess, and it made a lasting impression on me. To this day, I will not watch horror movies or read scary books.

Back when I was very young, I remember that trucks and carts selling fruits and vegetables came around regularly through the alley. The drivers would yell out their arrival, and women would go to the truck, pick out what they needed, weigh the produce on a hanging scale, bag it, and pay the driver. There were no credit cards or charge accounts; payments were all cash.

Then there were other wheeled wagons called pushcarts coming through, and again the women would go out to the alley, bring their knives and scissors for sharpening on the pushcart wheel.

Today we all have refrigerators in our houses, but I do remember when I was very young, we had ice boxes and the "ice man" would come through the alley with wagons, selling big blocks of ice. They would grab the ice with a giant pincher, heave the big block over their shoulder, and bring it into the house. They wore a black rubber-like apron so that melting ice wouldn't get them wet. The big opening at the top of the icebox was for the block of ice, and at the bottom, the large tray, a drip tray, collected the water from the melting ice.

They sold ice by the pound, and the way we indicated how much we needed was to put the ice company's red card in a window. The card had numbers, indicating on the side of the card if we wanted 10, 15, 20 or 25 pounds. We'd stand the card face up showing the number of pounds we wanted. I used to see that at my grandparent's house. By the time my parents had bought their own home, it came with an electric refrigerator.

(When Al and I bought our first house on Wilson and Richmond, it came with an electric refrigerator. I remember that the unit on top fascinated me because I thought it looked like a big wedding cake; of course, it was the operating part of the box. I guess I had weddings and wedding cakes on my mind.)

Later on, our family divided. I stayed with my Aunt Carrie (my mother's sister) and my two cousins, Sally and Jackie, in their apartment on Diversey and Kedzie. My sister stayed with my mother (I don't remember where), and my dad stayed at his mother's home.

When my father finally got a job, we all got back together again, and my dad finally got his beloved Buick. Things were beginning to look up again.

I started kindergarten at Pierce Elementary School in that neighborhood. It was the middle of the Depression and my father lost his job again, so we had to move in with my paternal grandparents, Jenny and Robert Sapero, who had a huge apartment in Wicker Park. My father's two sisters, Aunt Miriam and Aunt Lil, who were not married at that time, lived there also.

# Grammar School Days

I started attending Pierce School in Wicker Park but only kindergarten. Somehow, my next memory is when my father got a job, and we moved to our own apartment a block away from Moya and Grandpa. We lived on the third floor of an apartment building, at the corner of Spaulding and Barry. I remember it looked down into a courtyard.

After school, Laverne and I spent a lot of time at my grandmother's house because our parents were both working.

I transferred to Avondale School in the Logan Square neighborhood and remained in that school until I graduated eighth grade in 1939. I made a number of friends at Avondale, and at one time, we formed a girls' club that we named Sacajawea from the poem about Miles Standish. There also was a radio show about Sacajawea, the Indian maiden. And I think it was possible to form clubs through the radio. Our club—mostly the girls I went to grammar school with and later into high school—would meet regularly.

We even had a raffle, and the prize was a waffle iron. I don't recall why we had a raffle or why we were raising money. My mother bought most of the tickets, and we won the raffle. That was the first time I won something. Later I won a spelling bee at the Logan Movie Theater, and the prize was a pass for one week to see movies as often as they changed (which was three times a week).

Some of my Avondale friends were Marilyn Palmer (I used to sing in a trio with her), Gertrude Evers, Effie and Jenny Geanopolous, and my Polish friends, Charlotte Lasitchka and Regina Litmanski. This was mostly a Polish neighborhood, and I remember only one Jewish girl, Esther Sher.

*Girlfriends*

My memories of Avondale School included how we celebrated various holidays. On February 14, Valentine's Day, we sent paper valentines to kids in our class that we liked. If you didn't get a lot of valentines, it made you feel bad. Every Halloween in the evening, the school built a gigantic bonfire on the playground, and, wearing our costumes, we would parade around the fire showing them off. We

*There I am in grammar school at Avondale School.*

didn't have store-bought costumes in those days, but we all got creative using old clothes, funny hats, wigs, and whatever we found that we could put together and call it a costume. We would be judged and win prizes. It was just a tradition, but it was loads of fun. We competed in little contests, like dunking for apples.

I remember at Avondale School when we were on the playground and the bell would ring, we would have to line up. The girls would be in a separate line from the boys. Is that the way they still do it?

I even remember the names of a couple of my teachers. One was Ms. Johnson. I remember her because she was the youngest, prettiest, and nicest teacher in the whole school, and we all fell in love with her. And there was our eighth grade teacher, Miss Ady, a meanie who had a sour face all the time, but she was a good teacher.

Every day on my way to school, which was a block and a half away, I had to pass a shoe repair store. That was where I encountered my first taste of anti-Semitism because the owner would come out and yell anti-Jewish words at me.

It was the height of the Depression, and my father lost his job again. At that point, we had to leave our own apartment and split up our family. My father moved back with his parents, my mother and Laverne moved in with Moya, and I moved in with Aunt Carrie and my cousins, Sally and Jackie. They lived in a yellow brick building on the corner of Diversey and Kedzie. We all went to Avondale School. I don't recall how long I stayed with them.

*That's my cousin Sally and me, maybe at summer camp. I grew very fast. I was always the largest one in grammar school. I guess that was the reason I was so shy. If we put on a play, I always played the part of a king or some other male. I didn't like the way I looked; I wanted to be a five-foot-two blonde with blue eyes.*

At Avondale School, my mother was very active in the Parent Teacher Association (PTA); she was vice president. The PTA used to meet in the school basement once a month and they would serve coffee. I could smell the coffee, and the aroma was so delicious to me, even though I was only twelve or thirteen years old. But it smelled so good. Once I asked my mother if I could taste her coffee. It had cream and sugar in it, and it tasted awful. I guess that's why today I like black coffee because of the aroma.

I remember that we did not move from class to class as we did in high school. In eighth grade, we stayed in the same classroom for the whole day. That teacher taught everything. We did not have a separate teacher for math, English, music, history, and geography. So, when I went to high school—I'd never been in the high school building before—it was somewhat scary. The kids today have been in their high schools practically from first grade to participate in all kinds of activities. But we didn't. Our high school was so big, and we moved from class to class and had different teachers for different subjects. It was brand new to me. I loved it, though, after I got used to it.

Another memory when I was much younger was being on a swing on the playground. Two kids could ride the same swing facing each other. I think I fell off the swing, and my grandmother Moya rushed over to me. The swing almost hit her.

Across the street from Avondale School was the candy store. They had school supplies as well as candy, and that was a hangout place for me. The store, known as a "two-step," was up two steps to get into it. That was a great place to buy candy, a little licorice, three-for-a-penny, and all the other wonderful penny candy stuff. I think every grammar school has a place like that.

(When we lived in Skokie, my boys would ride their bikes to Key Pharmacy and buy comic books and candy bars; then they would go next door to Peck's Hardware to get a ten-cent Coke in a glass bottle from the Coke machine.)

When I was about nine or ten, the school offered piano lessons for about twenty-five cents a lesson. We didn't have an actual piano in those days, but they gave us a cardboard keyboard, and that's how I began. Along with playing on cardboard, I learned to read music. Later on, my Aunt Miriam had an old upright piano, and she gave it to me. I loved playing and I graduated to better teachers. I remember one teacher wouldn't let me play pieces I already knew, like Rachmaninoff; she made me go back to exercises and simple etudes. I was not happy.

Every year, we would have a recital to which parents and friends were invited. In one recital, there were about ninety students performing their one piece. Because my last name began with "S," my turn to play was eightieth. My poor father sat patiently through the first seventy students, and after my turn, he left and waited in the lobby.

In August of 1937, Chicago had the worst polio outbreak in its history with about a hundred new cases every day. The schools postponed their opening indefinitely. A dream come true for kids? Hardly. Radio stations

*I was probably about twelve or thirteen in this picture.*

*This is our family—my dad, my mom, Laverne, and me. Yes, I was as tall as my father was. I grew tall way ahead of everyone else.*

broadcasted lessons for each grade level for home study. The lessons were only fifteen minutes long. Most parents would not let their kids out of the house, and even if they did, they could not go to theaters, pools, and playgrounds. This lasted for four weeks, and schools reopened, although most of us didn't return until our parents were sure the epidemic was over.

PATRICIA SMITH (FROM LEFT), CHUCK MURRAY, JIM MURRAY AND JACK SMITH LISTENING TO RADIO LESSONS, SEPT. 13, CHICAGO

*Polio outbreak, Chicago, 1937*

# *Childhood Fun*

*This is a picture of Laverne, my cousin Dick, and me, but the rest of the people in this picture are their friends. I'm the one with the messy hair. Laverne, I think, is down in front.*

In the summer, for a couple of years when finances were better, we all—my mom, Laverne, Aunt Carrie, Sally, Jackie, and I—used to go to a farm in Knox, Indiana, for a one or two-week vacation. My dad would drive down along with Uncle Harry. What did we do there? We took a trip one time to Culver Military Academy, which is right near this farm. And on the farm, we would pick stuff and watch them milk the cows. I remember seeing big blocks of something white in the barn that the cows used to lick. I was always very curious, so I decided to try it. I licked it and found out the hard way that it was just a big block of salt. On the farm, we rode around in a funny little truck that the farmer's wife (they called her "mamashana") would drive. The truck had an open back with seats on each side of the back along its length. It was an older truck and was kind of fun.

Somebody also had a car that we rode called a "roadster," and the best part was that it had a rumble seat, which was an extra seat in the back where a trunk usually was. We had a great time there.

Everybody in those days used to go to the movie theaters. For example, my grandmother Moya was a big fan of free movie dishes or whatever they were giving away. She went to the movie theater and got a dish each night or lipstick or a dresser set (a mirrored tray with a comb and a brush). Everybody got something just for going. Moya collected an entire set of matching dishes that way. That was the height of luxury, having matching dishes or silverware. Everybody had hand-me-down dishes, so a matched set was very special.

I was a big, big movie fan. It used to cost ten cents to go to the movies, and they changed three times a week. Friday was one of the changing days, Tuesday was another, and I think Sunday was yet another. I loved going to the movies, and I didn't particularly want to go with anyone else. I didn't want to have people talking at me. I just wanted to be alone in the movie theater. I would go every time they changed films.

Movie theaters, in addition to giving away dishes for the adults, would have special events for the kids on Saturday afternoons. After the feature film, they would turn off the projector, turn on the house lights, and have events on the stage—spelling bees, pie-eating contests, and apple bobbing. And if you won, you got a one-week movie pass. I won a couple of spelling bees and was in my glory. I went as many times as I could, even if that meant seeing the same film twice. A cartoon and a newsreel were included in the movie package. I loved every minute of it.

One of the cowboy stars I remember was Tom Mix. Sometimes it was a double feature, two full-length pictures, and they always had short subjects. Robert Benchley was one of my favorite short subject stars, and the shorts ran about twenty minutes. His son Peter Benchley has written many popular novels.

This was way before television. Listening to radio, going to the movies, and reading books were the main entertainment activities.

Remember everyone we knew had no money due to the great Depression. Three other things I loved to do were walking, singing, and reading. I used to walk from Albany Park all the way to Logan Square by myself. No one was afraid to walk alone; we did it all the time.

I remember something else: the first Superman comic book came out in 1938. There were other ones, and I remember buying them for ten cents. That's all I can tell you. And then a million other comic books began being printed. I read recently that the first Superman comic book sold for $3.2 million. I should have kept it!

Then, there was a very popular magazine that had been around since 1905, starting out as the *Monthly Story Blue Book* magazine and later changing to just *The Blue Book*. It was printed on cheap paper, like comic books, sold for a dime and was very popular; everyone read it. It featured stories written by Edgar Rice Burroughs, Booth Tarkington, Zane Grey, and Agatha Christie. *The Blue Book* magazine featured novels and short stories. It ceased publishing in 1975, but I don't know why. Around that time, paperback books started appearing and they cost a quarter.

I was a very shy person, preferring a good book to anything else—books and movies and, oh, yes, music. I sang in any choir I could find. I knew how to read music from my piano lessons. My grandmother had a beautiful voice and so did my mother. The story goes that my grandmother received an offer to sing on stage, but in her days, people did not consider theaters the proper place for young women.

We all lived together for several years. Sally and I slept in an unheated back porch, sharing a twin bed. We had a coal-burning furnace in the basement that heated the house, and we were so poor that my dad used to go through the ashes in the furnace to look for any unburned coals (he called "clinkers") so we could use them again. I remember how we played a Bingo game on the radio, which was produced by the A&P grocery chain, and winning a bag of groceries that kept us going for a while.

# High School: 1939–1943

I graduated from Avondale School in the Logan Square neighborhood in January 1939, having skipped a grade in grammar school, and started Roosevelt High School from the house we shared with Aunt Carrie, Sally, Jackie and baby Ronnie. I remember how excited I was when the first day of high school came. I had a new dress for the occasion, but when I opened the front door to go to school, the snow was so high I could not get out. School cancelled classes that day, and I was very sad.

I was in awe my first days at Roosevelt. It was so different from grammar school. We changed rooms for every course.

**DOROTHY S. SAPERO**
Section Head, Symphonic Choir; Mixed Chorus; Log Staff; Orientation Committee; Freshman Sponsor; Honor Society; Senior Council; Clerk, Office; Secretary; Library; Agent, Weekly; Lunch Guard; "Burthen"; G.A.A.; "My Pal"; Interroom Volleyball, Baseball; Readers' Round Table; J.Y.L.

*Me in the Roosevelt yearbook*

*My yearbook accomplishments*

When I started high school, my two best friends were Lyle Bass and Phyllis Lurie, now Goldberg. Phyllis's parents owned a jewelry store on Kedzie next to the L tracks.

I loved Roosevelt High School; in fact, I loved all my schools. It was located at the corner of Kimball and Wilson Avenues, and I walked a little over a mile every day to get there, no matter what the weather was. I remember we had to take swimming classes and pass a test before we could graduate. My first class as a freshman was swimming at 8:00 a.m. After walking the mile to school in below zero weather, I had to get into a cold swimming pool. I never forgot that.

One funny story about walking home from Roosevelt was when I was standing on the corner in front of the school, waiting to cross the street. All of a sudden, my underpants fell down to the ground. I guess the elastic broke or something. I was so embarrassed, I just stepped out of them, left them there on the sidewalk, and walked straight home! Roosevelt High School is still there, and their teams are still the Rough Riders.

I also always loved to sing. Moya and my mother also loved singing, and I learned many old songs from them. Therefore, when I started at Roosevelt High School, the first thing I did was to get into the choir. I think that was my only outside activity.

The best time of my life was being in school. Since I loved books so much, whenever I had a birthday, everyone knew to give me books. In those days, if you had a favorite character like Nancy Drew, you could buy books that had three novels in one binding. It was a big thick book, and I loved those. I used to get them all the time, so I had lots to read. That was my big thing.

I had several jobs during my high school years. The one I remember the most was on Milwaukee Avenue at the Lerner store. I don't know how it happened, but I ended up being the head cashier. That's when I learned about counting money, filling out forms, and making sure all the numbers balanced. Lerner's was a large chain of women's clothing. Later, I worked at another one at Belmont and Lincoln. It was fun.

In high school, my favorite classes were of course English, reading famous literature like *A Tale of Two Cities* and many Shakespearean plays. I loved it all. And I enjoyed singing in the symphonic choir, conducted by John Hamilton. I didn't sing in the girls' chorus; ours was a mixed choir of girls and boys.

I also loved chemistry. I wanted a chemistry set when I was a little girl. A toy store was right next to the temple that we attended. I actually went to Hebrew school and Sunday school, but I never cared for it. I learned to read some Hebrew, but I don't remember it anymore. But in the toy store window was a Gilbert chemistry set. I wanted that so badly, but my parents couldn't afford it. Later on, when I was an adult with my own money, I actually bought myself a Gilbert chemistry set and made ink. I thought it was great fun. I think that's why I like to cook and bake because I have to measure ingredients. I just love doing that and turning it into something else.

I wasn't crazy about math, though I got good grades. In high school, we were graded A, B, C, D, E, but in grammar school, it had been S, E, F for superior, excellent, failure. I always received good grades.

I didn't have any boyfriends. I wasn't at all interested in them, and they weren't interested in me. Later, when I was in college, I had a date, but it was horrible. It was because I belonged to a sorority at Northwestern and was supposed to be one of the beauty queens wearing a long white dress and carrying red roses. Somehow, I had met a guy who was in the ROTC. He took me to the beauty pageant as his date, but I did not like him. Going up the stage stairs in my long dress and carrying the roses, I tripped. I was somewhat klutzy. The whole idea of sororities did not appeal to me, and I didn't stay with it.

We did participate in the Jewish holidays because our family was observant, but we were not very religious. We were the kind of Jewish people who would never have bacon or pork in the house, but it was OK if we ordered it in a restaurant. I could never understand that point of view. When you're a certain age, you take things very seriously. Whenever I heard the national anthem playing on the radio, I would stand up in its honor. I tried to get involved with Judaism for a while, but I lost interest in that and am still not that interested.

I took Spanish, chemistry, bookkeeping, shorthand, typing, advanced English, history, and other college prep subjects. I took the shorthand, bookkeeping, and typing classes with the realization that in order to afford college, I would have to have skills in order to earn money. World War II started in 1941, and it was still on when I graduated. In those days, we had two graduations a year. My graduation was in January of 1943. These days, graduations are always in June.

# Post–High School/College

We were in the middle of World War II when I was in high school and after graduation. I got a civil service job working for the U.S. Fifth Army Ordnance Division in the First National Bank Building at Dearborn and Monroe. I was an excellent typist and very good at shorthand. What's "shorthand?" You could look it up on Wikipedia, but it was a system of symbols. A stenographer could turn spoken words into written symbols quickly to capture conversations or narratives. It was an early form of recording. Court reporters were very good at this. There were two different methods of shorthand—Gregg or Pitman. I excelled in Pitman.

While working for the army, I eventually was transferred to a department that was working on training manuals used in the various war plants. They hired professors from various universities who were writing manuals for the workers in the various war plants. I took dictation from them and typed up the manuals. I was very good at it. I just fell into that kind of job, and it was wonderful.

We developed a suggestion program for all the workers in various factories. When I first started with the army, I was in a typing pool in a huge room with little tiny desks. Every desk had a typewriter, and we sat there all day, typing. I remember we had to use carbon paper between the white sheets in order to get multiple copies. We'd type on the front page and put a sheet of carbon paper behind it, another white sheet, and another carbon paper sheet. I think three copies were all we could do at one time. We threw away the used carbon paper each time. Carbon paper was a very thin, onionskin kind of paper with a coating on the back that left marks on our hands each time we used them. In those days, we always wore dresses or skirts and blouses, and petticoats under our dresses. No girls wore slacks. When I would come home after work, I would find carbon paper purple marks on the inside of my petticoat.

That job was extremely boring, so when they needed somebody to work in the personnel office where they were creating these training manuals, somehow they sent me there and I loved it. These writers were very smart. One of the writers was the son of a big business owner in Chicago—a very famous name, Arvey, I think. I was very good at Pitman shorthand, and I would take dictation for the manuals.

Every factory had suggestion boxes in which employees could drop an idea about how to improve what they were doing. Whenever they emptied the suggestion boxes, they would send all of the suggestions to our office. I would type them up and give them to the committee that would go over them. I would meet with the committee and take the notes, and then they would pick out the winners who would each get a reward at a ceremony held for them. Overall, my work in the personnel department was really very, very interesting. After completing the training manuals, they would send them out to different plants.

During my days at the army, I also attended night school where I took college courses. To get there, I had to take two streetcars, but it worked out fine. I was trying to earn college credits, and the only thing that was a big mistake was deciding to take a four-hour lab class in biology. I'd get home each night after class after 10:00 p.m. and get up the next morning at 6:00 a.m. to get to my army job.

The laboratory course was terrible, but I took it for a couple of semesters, despite the long hours at night and the short hours I had to study and sleep. I was very serious about things.

During the war, there were free street shows performed daily all over downtown Chicago, selling war bonds. Some of these shows featured very big stars. At lunch, I would attend every one I could find. At night, I would be on the floor of our living room, exercising. My father said our downstairs neighbors would complain about the noise from my jumping jacks, but no one ever did.

After a year or so, I saved up enough money for tuition, and through dieting and exercise, I lost the weight I had wanted to lose. I had saved enough to go on to college, but the schools I loved the most were Stanford University in Palo Alto, California; Northwestern University in Evanston; and the University of Chicago. I wanted a school that had high ratings in academics, a place that would challenge me. I fell in love with Stanford, not only because it was located on a beautiful campus with the mountains behind it and the ocean in front, but also because it was sometimes called "the Harvard of the West." I applied to all three schools and was accepted at all of them. But I began thinking, Stanford, that's a long way away, I'd have to fly, it's expensive, and I wouldn't go home very often. I thought that it was not such a good plan after all. I realized that traveling to Palo Alto, California, would be too much of a financial drain on my hard-earned, limited funds.

I loved the academic challenges of University of Chicago, but traveling from the north side to the south side was a bit overwhelming. I finally decided to go to Northwestern's School of Speech in nearby Evanston and to major in radio. The School of Speech is now the School of Communications or something similar. I was disappointed in Northwestern. It seemed to me that it was more of a party school, but anyway that's where I was. And I did well there. Cloris Leachman, Paul Lynde, Charlton Heston, and other future stars were my classmates. I didn't start there as a freshman because I had credits from my night school years, so I started as a sophomore.

My girlfriend Lyle Bass, who had been my best friend all through high school, was also at Northwestern. Sometimes, we'd walk all the way to Howard Street and get on a bus. I really wanted to have the experience of living in a dormitory, and I didn't want to do the sorority thing, so I finally got a room in a campus dormitory. I planned to start living on campus during the next semester.

I was a little disappointed in NU because it did not offer the challenges I wanted. During my first year, having achieved my weight goal, I finally had perfect measurements and landed a job as a part-time fashion model at a dress manufacturing company. I soon discovered that modeling was for idiots; I might as well have been a dummy in a store window.

*Here I am posing in front of some tavern. Ha! Ha! What a terrible pose! I was skinny then.*

# *Bicycling and Other Adventures*

**Trip with girlfriends**

I did not know how to ride a bike, but I thought I'd like it. I saw an ad for a cheap balloon-tire used bike, bought it for $10, and learned how to balance and ride it. I found out about the American Youth Hostels (AYH), an international organization that had started in Europe. I joined it with one of my girlfriends, Phyllis Lurie, and we used to go on some of their local bike trips. Before I got the bike, I had gone on some walking trips with them. The premise of AYH was that you had to get to your destination under your own power—no motorized vehicles—whether it was walking or bicycling. They said horseback riding was acceptable, but I don't see how that would be under your own power.

For seventy-five cents a night, we could stay at youth hostel cabins. The closest one was in Des Plaines at the Methodist Campgrounds about 10 miles away. They provided a bed, but we brought our own linens or made a kind of sleeping bag out of muslin. They had pots, pans, dishes, and silverware, and we cooked our own meals. I loved it!

Later on, I became more adventurous and took longer bike trips with an older friend of mine, Lois, who was a writer for the *Chicago Daily News* (not in existence any more). One time, we took our bikes on a train to Boston, and when we got there, we stayed in a hotel called the Parker House. Yes, that's where Parker House rolls were created. We stayed there for a couple of nights and toured Boston. Then we took our bikes on a ferry to the tip of Cape Cod in Provincetown. We rode down the whole length, about sixty miles, stopping in little towns along the way.

Before we left Provincetown on our way to Hyannisport, Lois told me to buy a sketchpad and some charcoal. "What for?" I asked. She said, "You'll see." And it turned out that while we were riding, we would get off our bikes, sit by the side of the road, and try sketching. The buildings were very unusual with their widows' walks on top of the houses. As the story goes, the sailors' wives used to go up there and watch and wait for their sailor-husbands to come home. So I tried sketching for the first time ever in my life. It was amazing to see what I had done. There was no one to criticize me, and the sketches came out amazingly well. I was really hooked on art for a while, and I'm glad I had that experience.

We rode until we reached the bottom of the cape, which was the town of Hyannisport. Then we took our bikes on a ferry to the island of Nantucket and stayed in a cottage located right on the ocean. I remember picking and eating fruit, which they called "beach plums." The towns had cobblestone streets that were no fun for bike riders.

After Cape Cod, I went to California to see the Pacific Coast. My Aunt Sarah's sister Jean lived in Los Angeles, and she said I should call her when I got there, but first I wanted to find a place to stay. It was a long train ride to Los Angeles, and when I arrived, I went to the information desk at the train station. They recommended a hotel, so I took a cab and went there. It was quite noisy, and when I looked out the window of the hotel, I saw a number of men in cars, picking up women on the street. I didn't know it was in the red light district, but I spent the night there. I called Aunt Sarah's sister in the morning, and she said, "Oh, you can't stay there." She came downtown and took me to her house. She was a health nut and made these healthy juices. She'd grind fruits and vegetables in the morning and end up with a glass of green stuff, kind of strange for me. But it wasn't bad.

*This is a picture from left to right, Aunt Sarah's sister Jean, my mother, and Aunt Sarah.*

# *Self Improvement*

**Working**

I was always overweight, and when I was in high school, I decided to change everything. I went on a very good diet while I was working for the army downtown.

I was determined to 1) save up all my paychecks so I could go to college, and 2) lose weight so I could get a job as a model. I took diet sandwiches to work (on Rye Crisp) and had just enough change for carfare and a drink. My dad asked me one time, "What if you lose a penny? What would you do?" After that, I began carrying an extra nickel.

The bank had a free giant scale in their lobby, and I'd weigh myself every day. I would eat my Rye Crisp sandwiches, which by then were rather soggy, but I learned to love them.

I saved every penny and lost the weight I had wanted to lose. My dream was to get to the point where I would have perfect dimensions, and when I was at Northwestern, I got a job modeling for a clothing manufacturer who used me to model all their new designs before they decided to manufacture them. I was proud of getting into modeling shape, but I finally decided that modeling was one of the stupidest jobs one could get, but I was paid and saved the money. I was about nineteen or twenty at the time.

I used to exercise like crazy. We had a third-floor apartment and a big radio console in the living room. I would lie down on the floor and hook my hands around the legs of the console radio and do rolling exercises, go back and forth, and do jumping jacks. My father would say, "You're going to break the floor and the neighbors won't like it. You make all that noise." But that's what I did to reach my goal.

Years later, my kids knew about my obsession with dieting and sometimes teased me about it, but they became aware of their own weight problems and kind of followed my lead. I almost became a vegetarian.

I also was extremely shy and unsure of myself. Certain memories remain with me.

*This photo of me was hand-colored. I was fascinated with paints that I could put on pictures. I once received a whole set of them and colored everything.*

In fourth or fifth grade, the teacher asked a question that nobody answered. I knew the answer but was too bashful to say anything. Instead, I mouthed the answer, which the teacher saw. "That's right, Dorothy," she said and I blushed.

Another time I wrote a play about the rescue of a cat from a tree—I was in fifth grade—and my teacher, without telling me, entered it in a contest promoted by the Red Cross. To my utter amazement, I won the first prize, $1 and a certificate, which I received at an assembly. I could have "died" of mortification, but secretly I was proud.

As I grew and matured, I became involved in many exciting experiences and gradually lost some of my shyness, but it wasn't until I was in my fifties that I found myself thrust into a position that suddenly brought forth abilities I didn't know I had. I became more and more self-assured and spoke publicly on subjects I knew and believed in. It was a long time coming, but I have found myself speaking aloud and expressing my opinion, even if nobody asked. In my eighties, I even started a blog called "Listen to Dotty." I also have decided to stop "dieting," eat normally, and forget my dream of being "5'2" with eyes of blue." After all, I am over 5'2" and my eyes are hazel brown. Ah, well!

# Early TV Days

When I was a student at Northwestern, I picked up a copy of the September 1944 edition of *Mademoiselle*, a popular woman's magazine, and read a story about a group of girls running a television station in Chicago. TELEVISION—What the heck was that? It was defined as a cross between movies and radio—my two favorite subjects. I was so intrigued that I did a little research and found out that Balaban & Katz, the owners of Chicago's major motion picture theaters, owned a television station on the top floor of the State-Lake building. It was the first television station in Chicago and the third in the nation, and it started when there were only two hundred sets in the whole city.

I called and got an appointment with the vice president. His office was in the Chicago Theater building upstairs, so that's where I went for the interview. I was so innocent; I took my mother with me! I remember the two of us sitting there for the interview.

That's when my life changed. They offered me a job at station WBKB, which was across State Street above the State Lake Theater.

I remember asking one of my professors at the School of Speech if I should drop out of Northwestern and take the job. His response was something like, "Television is just a fad and will never go any place. Stay in school!" He was a fairly well known professor, and I found out later he taught TV classes!

WBKB hired me for $25 a week and all the movie passes I wanted, gave me a uniform, and made me a member of the all-girl crew of ten. We ran the station under the direction of Beulah Zachary and Katherine (Kit) Carson. We did everything except operate the transmitter. We had two male engineers for that.

That is, we operated the TV cameras, sound, and the projector

*Some of the all-girl crew at WBKB-TV*

showing movies. We built sets, developed new programs, and directed them. When we showed films, we removed the lens from the projector and shot directly into the camera. With all the free passes, I could go to all the theaters downtown any time I wanted. I thought I'd stay out of school for just one semester, but I never went back.

When I first started at WBKB, I was a dolly pusher. The cameras (kinescopes) were mounted on platforms with wheels that we dolly pushers would move according to what the director of the show wanted. We wore earphones and got our instructions that way. The camera girls would be the ones adjusting the lenses for close-ups, etc. They rode on the dollies with the cameras. Many a time, we'd go to one of the downtown theaters with our free passes and study the lighting, camera angles, music, etc. of the Hollywood movies, and then we'd try to duplicate some of them with the TV cameras.

We had a huge music library of transcriptions, which were large 16" vinyl records with different "cuts" on each. I remember deciding to listen to every cut and classify it as "suspense music" or "happy music" or "sad." I never did finish that project. It was a good idea because music would sometimes set the scene. After being a dolly pusher, I graduated to the sound booth, operating the mikes, turntable, etc. Then I began directing and writing and coming up with show ideas. No one knew much about television. Here is the history as I researched it:

> Contrary to popular opinion, television was not a phenomenon of the twentieth century. Even in biblical times, some people predicted that the day would come when it would be possible to see things that were happening far away. Beginning in 1884 and later in 1877, there were proposals for crude mechanical systems. However, few, if any of these early discoveries are in use in modern TV. Not until Philo Farnsworth, an American inventor, developed the first working television system with electronic scanning in 1928 did the development of today's TV begin. It proved that light could be converted into electrical impulses that were transmitted and then converted back to their original optical form. Farnsworth, at the age of fourteen, worked out the principle of the image-dissector television camera. As a farm boy, he said his inspiration for scanning lines of the cathode ray tube came from the back-and-forth motion used to plow a field. The early scanning was around 30 to 40 lines per second, but today scanning is at 525 lines. A tremendous amount of history and theories were put forth over the years before we arrived at television as we know it

Television in Chicago really began when motion picture czars, Barney Balaban, head of Paramount Pictures, and his brother, John, head of the theater chain Balaban & Katz, applied for and received a license from the Federal Communications Commission (FCC) to operate an experimental TV station. Its call letters were W9XBK. Balaban & Katz had more than one hundred theaters in the Chicago area and was a subsidiary of Paramount Pictures. Thus, Paramount not only produced the films but also controlled the theaters playing them, allowing them complete control over distribution and presentation of their product. Paramount ran more than one thousand five hundred theaters in the United States, plus more in Canada, Europe, and parts of South America.

But around 1948, the U.S. Department of Justice didn't like this monopoly and ordered Paramount and other producers to decide whether they wanted to be in film production or theater ownership business. Barney Balaban (Paramount) chose to remain in the production business, and his brother John stayed with theater ownership.

Having lived in Chicago my whole life, I knew that the Balaban & Katz theaters were legends for the beautiful "movie palaces" they operated. Here's a picture of the Chicago Theater, their flagship building.

When I was a kid, we frequented the small neighborhood theaters, but on special occasions, my parents took us to the magnificent Harding Theater on Milwaukee Avenue. On first walking in, it was noticeably very special: quiet and beautiful. The carpeting was so thick that we almost sank into it, and we whispered when we spoke.

Around 1939, John Balaban convinced his brother at Paramount that Balaban & Katz should apply for a television license. They applied to the FCC and received their experimental license. They

*Chicago Theater*

turned the upper three floors of the State Lake Theater building into their idea of a TV station. Then they realized they knew nothing about how to operate a station. They hired Bill Eddy, an ex-submarine captain, who was partially deaf.

Eddy had worked with Philo Farnsworth and later with RCA and had invented many electronic devices and lighting techniques, which are still in use today. They asked him to

*Captain Bill Eddy*

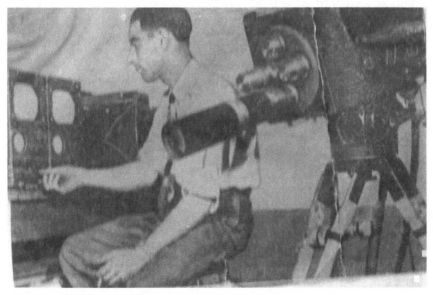

*Dick Shapiro, WXBK/WBKB engineer*

start WXBK with a budget of $60,000. He quickly assembled his staff: chief engineer, Arch Brolly, whom he knew from his days with Philo Farnsworth; Reinald Werrenrath, who worked with him at NBC; and from Chicago, Bill Kusack and Dick Shapiro, TV repairmen who had worked for RCA Victor, and they started telecasting in 1940.

Around the same time, Chicago-based Zenith also had an experimental license and were telecasting but mostly test patterns. Both of these stations had about a fifteen-mile range. The Zenith station was primarily interested in developing subscription non-commercial television, which they thought would be the true future of TV. After December 7, 1941, the FCC ordered all experimental stations off the air, and they had to go dark. They announced that any experimental station could replace their license with a commercial license and be on the air at least four hours a day. Zenith said no, but B&K said yes.

Captain Eddy and his engineers "jury-rigged" something that met the FCC's approval. They built two homemade cameras, including the mounts, which Eddy fashioned from old barber's chairs. He rigged them with small motors to raise and lower the cameras, and in 1943, W9XBK became WBKB, Chicago's first commercial television station. That's the station where I worked. After the war, Zenith renewed their license and tried to develop its Phonevision pay-TV service. It was not successful and did not last.

At the same time, Capt. Eddy, along with B&K, knowing that

*Navy Radio School 1942*

the navy would need trained radar personnel, offered his staff and two of the three floors of W9XBK for a radar training school. Originally estimated to train 135 radar technicians, the total came closer to 86,000.

I reported for work in the State Lake building at 190 N. State in the spring of 1945. At the drugstore at State and Lake, I would have coffee with guests and announcers from the station, including Russ Mitchell (who announced wrestling from Rainbow Arena, or "Whispering" Joe Wilson who announced bowling by whispering). After Capt. Eddy turned over two of the three floors to the navy, WBKB's only space was the twelfth floor. There was a bridge between the State-Lake building into the next building south. On the street level, there was the marquee of the State-Lake Theater, a Riecks Beanery restaurant, and a couple of small stores. (Now, there is a Potbelly restaurant, the glass windows of ABC-TV, etc.) Below the studios and the radar school were the showrooms of furriers. I met Capt. Bill Eddy on that first day.

Once, when Esther, one of the camera operators, had a problem with her lens, she got off the platform and went around to the front to

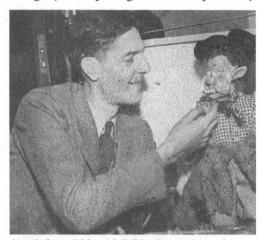

*Here's Capt. Eddy with "Lil Joe," an animated puppet who could smoke a cigarette.*

*I began as a dolly pusher. This is a picture of a camera mounted on the rolling platform called a dolly.*

*Note the high voltage power supply on the platform in the front.*

*There were about nine or ten on the crew and two or three women directors. Here's the whole crew from 1946. I'm in the front row.*

*Our directors were Beulah Zachary and Kit Carson. Here is Kit Carson.*

Helen Carson, television director and producer, gets to work in the studio prepar- to put a show on the air. Here, with series...

jiggle it. By accident, she stepped right onto that power supply, and the voltage knocked her clear across the studio. The program was live, so the other camera stayed on the set and the show went on. She was OK.

I loved working there. On the first day, I pushed that dolly for programs that included the Albright twins, famous for their *Picture of Dorian Gray* film and painting; the head of the Chicago Health Department about medical issues (another one of my interests); and a quiz show for Commonwealth Edison. Here I am running the camera.

At that time, some businesses would produce simple shows just

*Our two main camera operators were Rachel Stewart, shown here, and Esther Rajeski.*

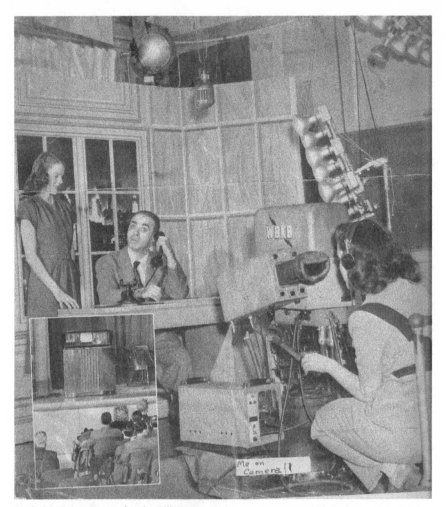

*Me behind the camera for the Bill Anson program*

to get practice for the future. Many local announcers and performers would do the same. That first day was so exciting that I couldn't stop talking about it when I went home. I told my parents that someone should print a listing of all the shows so people would know what was on. (I could have been the one to start *TV Guide*.) There was no formal schedule; only that we had to be on the air at least four hours a day.

I quickly learned how to operate the cameras, work the sound equipment, help build sets, and give studio tours. When we didn't have anything to telecast, a couple of us would play checkers for the camera, or they would point the camera out a window and show the river,

*VARIETY*

Wednesday, May 7, 1947

REMEMBER THE DAYS
With Dave Garroway, Helen Malone
Director: Kit Carson
Writer: Dorothy Sapero
30 Min.: Tuesday, 8 p.m. (CDT)
Sustaining
                          Dorothy Spero
in writing the script used fine re-
straint in not hoking the material,
letting the viewers make their own
comments.

*I got reviews even if they misspelled my name in one place! —Variety*

**CHILDREN WILL SING OPERA CARMEN**
The All Children's Grand Opera Company will present "Car-
men" at 3:15 p.m. June 9 in the auditorium of Lane Tech-
nical High School. Leads, left to right, include Bonnie
Roberts, 9; Sheldon Patinken, 10; Bunny Rose, 9, and Ira
Lee, 10.

*Quiz Kids in Carmen*

traffic, Chicago Theater across the street, whatever. We were able to develop our own programming ideas and put them on the air.

I once read about a children's production of *Carmen*, and I contacted them and got them to perform for us. It turned out that most of the kids were former *Quiz Kids* (a popular radio show of the time) and one ten year old, Sheldon Patinkin, became one of the founders of Second

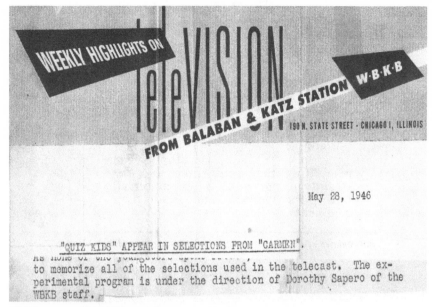

WEEKLY HIGHLIGHTS ON teleVISION FROM BALABAN & KATZ STATION W·B·K·B

190 N. STATE STREET · CHICAGO 1, ILLINOIS

May 28, 1946

"QUIZ KIDS" APPEAR IN SELECTIONS FROM "CARMEN".

to memorize all of the selections used in the telecast. The experimental program is under the direction of Dorothy Sapero of the WBKB staff.

*WBKB promo of kids' Carmen show*

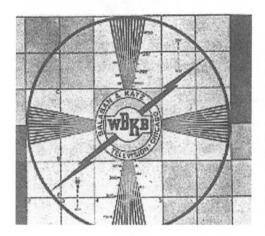

*Test pattern: Every day we would sign on with a test pattern and Offenbach's music. To this day, whenever I hear his Gaite Parisienne and Can-Can music (we used both, one for sign-on and one for sign-off), I'm carried back to those days.*

City and is the cousin of Mandy Patinkin, the film, TV, and movie star.

Television in Chicago was virtually unknown to the public. There were approximately three hundred sets in the city, owned mostly by engineers who pretty much had built them from kits. When the war ended, television sets began to sell, but the picture tubes were extremely small, and some companies offered a magnifying glass kind of cover to put in front of the tube. There were other gadgets to try to enlarge the picture. Today, it's very "in" to have a small picture like on the iPhone or an extremely large picture found on the TV projection units.

Another type used the end of the tube but added a mirror to project the picture up to the screen (supposedly a better image). Antennas, in those days, were known as "rabbit ears," and sometimes people would use a wire hanger that they straightened out for the antennas. Many times, someone would stand alongside the set, moving the antenna back and forth until they got a good image.

Originally, B&K had built a three-studio layout, but when Eddy turned over most of this space to the navy radar school, all that remained was a

*Courtesy Du.*

DIRECT-VIEWING RECEIVER. 20-INCH TUBE

*The first console sets were either a direct viewing type as shown by this 20" Dumont where the picture was actually the end of the viewing tube.*

*Here's the WBKB studio and control room.*

16x24-foot floor with single story height.

We used several ceiling and strip lighting units in a show. This is the lighting control board. The cables permitted adjustment of the ceiling lights both up and down and side to side. Later, they added other kinds of lighting such as spots and high intensity arc lights, but our studio did not have these. The heat of these lights was so intense that I remember during a children's Christmas choral concert where the kids were on risers, one or two fainted while being televised. Remember everything was live.

Another time, during a whodunit show, the leading man was to go to a sideboard and pour himself a drink from a decanter of wine, supposedly poisoned by the villain in the story. In order to highlight

*The kind of cameras used in those days, the kinescope, required a lot of light. These were the ceiling units. Each unit had twelve 300-watt reflector lamps.*

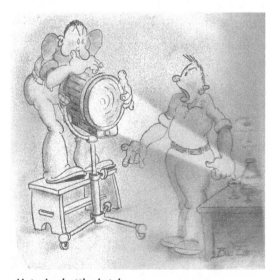

*Hot wine bottle sketch*

this decanter against the dark background of the set, extra lights focused on the bottle. During the entire act, the light poured its hot beam on the bottle. When the hero finally went to the table, poured his drink, and tossed off the now near-boiling liquid, he staged a dying scene rarely equaled. He actually had steam coming out of his mouth.

We had fancy dinner scenes where the candles would melt in front of our eyes, or a cooking show where the cook was perspiring and dripping beads of sweat into the pastry.

One time, we were televising a murder mystery show. At one point, the actor was to drink a glass of whiskey. When he began drinking, he grabbed his throat and said "Help, I've been poisoned," just like the script, but then he added, "I'm not kidding" and fell to the floor. It turned out that the prop person had not rinsed out the bottle before filling it with fake whiskey. Unfortunately, it contained carbon tetrachloride from a previous show. The actor recovered, and the prop person made sure to check her props more carefully in the future.

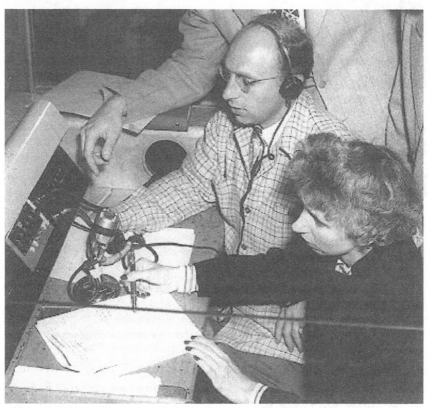

*Control booth—tiny, just big enough for an audio person, an engineer, the producer, and the director. It was hot and claustrophobic but it worked.*

(Could that have killed drinking for me? Who knows? I still don't like the taste or what it does to me. Now, I occasionally drink a dry wine when I'm out just to be sociable.)

*A newer, considerably larger control booth at another station*

*Transmitter where the engineers would send the show out over the airwaves*

While working at WBKB, I tried different ideas using this new medium. Once, I tried creating a 3-D effect using two cameras focused on one object, but I soon learned that 3-D was more complicated than that. But we were always thinking about the tremendous possibilities of television, and we were able to try out some of these ideas. We even tried our hand at creating some teaching programs (way ahead of our time).

Every show had to have titles, and here is how we created many of them, mostly through the inventive mind of Capt. Eddy. The simplest ones were on standard 11x14-inch neutral flat gray card stock—gray because white would have caused a reflection of white spots and flair. That is one reason why we advised actors and announcers not to wear white.

Sometimes the titles would be arranged billboard fashion, and the camera would pan across these boards.

There were many,

*My best friends at the station were Jerry Daly, a union projectionist who ran the films part-time at the station, and the engineers who kept the equipment working. I went out to eat with these wonderful men and spent many a night in the projection booths of various downtown movie houses with Jerry, watching him operate the huge 35mm projectors.*

*Preparing titles*

*Miniature title and credit billboard*

many other types mechanical titling. There were also mechanical attempts to create slow dissolves between pictures, do wipes, and create other fancy effects. These were the days before anyone could create these effects electronically.

WBKB can boast a bevy of "firsts." We had the first remote baseball game from Wrigley Field where the Cubs play. We were so proud that we had invited the press to watch the first-ever telecast of a ballgame. After the press arrived at the studio, we had them sit in a viewing room, and when the game started, we couldn't get the picture and tried to hide the television receiver! Later, we did successful remotes of wrestling from Rainbow Arena, harness racing from Washington Park, and, of course, baseball from both Cubs and White Sox parks.

When Russ Mitchell announced wrestling matches, Capt. Eddy, in his mahogany-paneled office, would provide sound effects into a mike on his desk. He'd snap a stalk of celery when a wrestler got an arm lock on his opponent or hit a

*Wrestling*

*Capt. Eddy's mobile unit #1 doing remotes*

cantaloupe with a hammer when they'd smack each other on the head with their fists. I remember that Capt. Eddy had this sign on the wall behind his desk.

One day, the top brass asked Capt. Eddy if he could do a family-oriented show. Capt. Eddy had worked with a young puppeteer at an RCA sales meeting in Bermuda. He was so impressed that he asked the

*Someone told me it translated into "Don't let the bastards wear you down."*

young man, Burr Tillstrom, if he could come to Chicago and work on this project. He did, adding a young actress, Fran Allison, and *Kukla, Fran & Ollie* was born.

Beulah Zachary was going to be the director and Lew Gomavitz (Gommy) would produce, but Beulah changed her mind after the first day because it was too claustrophobic in the control room, so Gommy took over as director and Beulah became the producer. Gommy di-

**Burr and puppets**

rected *Kukla, Fran & Ollie* from 1947 to 1957. Fran Allison had been on the radio show, *The Breakfast Club*, and Burr wanted her on his show. Burr had a traveling stage, and while those first shows had no script, *Kukla, Fran & Ollie* started talk-

**Kukla, Burr, Fran, and Ollie**

ing, and the material just gushed forth. The shows were an hour long, divided into four parts.

First, we brought kids who had birthdays up from the small audience to talk with Kukla and Ollie. Then there would be fifteen minutes with animals and a local trainer, fifteen minutes with another guest, and finally fifteen minutes with Fran just talking with Kukla and Ollie. Then they created other characters. Beulah Zachary became Beulah Witch. She worked closely with Burr, and her death in a plane accident was devastating to him and a blow to everyone. Jeanette

*Gommy, Kukla, Burr, and Beulah*

*Gommy, Beulah, Burr, and Fran*

was on the piano, playing their familiar theme music "Here We Go Again". The show became a national success.

On Sunday, March 29, 1986, the Museum of Broadcast Communications asked me to participate in a program honoring Burr Tillstrom. The event took place at the Chicago Historical Society in cooperation with WMAQ-TV.

The war ended in 1945, and radio stations around the country got their first TV licenses and began going on the air. In 1947 I received an offer for the position of film director for television station WTMJ-

# Burr Tillstrom
### 1917 — 1985

## Burr's Friends Remember
### PROGRAM

| | |
|---|---|
| *10:00 a.m.* | **"Kukla Kids Around"** — an episode of Kukla, Fran and Ollie. November 30, 1949. In person: Jim Conway and Dorothy Litwin remember Burr Tillstrom. |

*Program honoring Burr Tillstrom*

TV in Milwaukee. *The Milwaukee Journal* had its radio station WTMJ, and when the war ended, they wanted to begin television broadcasting. We were a group of young (I was twenty or twenty-one) women who were so-called "experts" in this new medium, and we received requests to help the many new stations going on the air around the country. My friend at the station, Elaine, went to Ohio, and another one of the girls went to Florida.

About that time, a newsreel company approached me and asked me to be part of a special on *Women in the News*. This is an excerpt from that film: https://youtu.be/Qp_T12tORKI

We went on the air in Milwaukee on December 3, 1947. It was the first television station in Wisconsin and the fifteenth commercial station in the United States. Its owner, the powerful *Milwaukee Journal*, had a very strong, established radio station, WTMJ. Both the radio and television station were located on Capital Drive, eight miles north of downtown Milwaukee. Walter Damn ran the entire enterprise—the newspaper, radio and TV station. (His staff knew him privately as the "great God damn.")

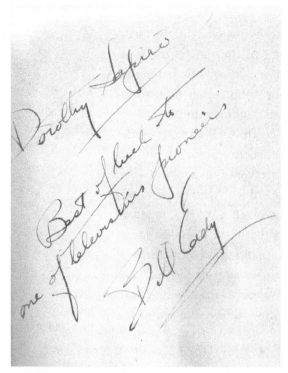

*Before I left BKB, Capt. Eddy autographed and gave me a copy of his book,* Television – The Eyes of Tomorrow.

As film director, I was encouraged to develop my own shows in addition to planning film programs. I began directing and writing shows because film distributors would

*WTMJ Sign – note the typo!*

not let us rent any of the Hollywood films. Therefore, I contacted Milwaukee's various industries, got some of their institutional films, and created shows based on the company's businesses. I met an elderly man, R.E. Aikens of

Waukesha, WI, who had been involved in the making of the movie *The Birth of a Nation*. His letter told me about other silent films we might acquire.

Thus began a series of silent movies with live interviews of people (when possible) who had been involved in some way with the film. As an aside, I planned to put *Birth of a Nation* on the air, but Walter Damn would not allow it. You can see in the

*Here I am at the microphone.*

# RADIO STATION WTMJ—The Milwaukee Journal

☐ COMMERCIAL
☐ SUSTAINING

Continuity for_____ MODERN MAGIC

Sunday, October 24, 1948-6:59-7:08:40        D. Sapero

Continuity for_____ THE CHILDREN'S CORNER        ☐ SUSTAINING

Friday, March 26, 1948        4:00—4:15 P.M.    D. Sapero
Presentation Date and Hour                Prepared by

*Scripts and shows I wrote*

**A MIRACLE OF POWER**

*Epoch Production Corporation*

March 13, 1948

Dorthy Sapero,
WTMJ-TV Film Director

Dear Miss Sapero:

        All those with TV sets out here were all set Friday nite to see the Birth so I have had much explaining to do. They were so disappointed.

        Thank you for your attention,

407 E. MICHIGAN STREET MILWAUKEE 2, WISCONSIN

PRODUCERS OF BIRTH OF A NATION

*Birth of a Nation letter*

last paragraph of Mr. Aiken's letter how disappointed he and his friends were when they found out it could not be aired.

Later, the station sent me to New York to arrange for films to show. I was only twenty-two and had never been to New York. I took my mother for her first trip (she paid her own way), and we not only had a wonderful time; we also arranged for many films.

While working in Milwaukee, I worked with visiting executives from various radio stations who were about to begin telecasting but didn't know how to do it.

In 1949 I received an offer from Hubbel Taft Jr., head of the newspaper and radio station in Cincinnati, Ohio, to join their staff at their new TV station, WKRC-TV. They signed on the air on April 4, 1949.

I left Milwaukee, went to Cincinnati, and began a new career as their film director. At that time, there were no taped shows, and the only way we could show a re-broadcast was to have it filmed and then shipped by air to all the stations for re-broadcasting. Thus, every day we would wait for the delivery of the film for airing that night. *WKRP*, the television show about a station in Cincinnati, had its basis,

*WTMJ's much larger studio*

*Here I am in the large projection room.*

I believe, on the real WKRC-TV where I worked. Again, I contacted local businesses and organizations and developed programming with them.

During that time, I met Al Litwin, my future husband, and I wanted to go back to Chicago where he was working at the Securities and Exchange Commission. I left Cincinnati after about a year and returned to Chicago where I worked for Malcolm Howard Advertising Agency (Jim Moran, the Courtesy Man, was one of our big accounts). I was involved in making commercials for him, and selecting and editing films. I also worked for Schwimmer Productions (*Man on the Street* and beauty pageants) and spent time selecting films for *The Jim Moran Show* at WGN-TV where my good friend, Jerry Daly, from my WBKB days, was working. Later I worked on the Chicago portion of *Your Show of Shows* with host Jack Carter.

The writers and I began work on the show at a small hotel in downtown Chicago, moved over to the Merchandise Mart mid-week into NBC studios for rehearsals, and ended up each week in the former Studebaker Theater in the Fine Arts Building on Michigan Avenue for airing the live broadcast. Guests on the show included Vincent Price, Martin and Lewis, and many, many more.

But that's another story...perhaps another time.

After my TV days, even before some of my sons were born, I had sent away for tickets to Bozo's Circus. We waited years for those tickets. When they finally came, we went. I remember walking into the studio, and some of the cameramen and engineers recognized me because I had worked with them at

*Ad for Your Show of Shows*

WBKB. Jim thought, Wow, my mother is really something. She was just my mother, but now she's important to all these guys that worked at Bozo's Circus and the TV station.

Jim missed his opportunity at the Bozo Buckets game (where kids threw a ball into six buckets to win prizes). "The girl next to me got the chance when the flashing arrow stopped on her," recalls Jim. "She was sitting right next to me. She missed the first bucket! I kept thinking to myself that I certainly would not have missed the first one, and most likely would have made at least three or four buckets. (We had been practicing at home for weeks.) I didn't understand how she could have missed all those buckets, and she was older than me, too."

# Meeting Al & Marriage

I never had been interested in boys, and when I went to high school, I was interested only in books, music, movies, and school—surely not boys. Also, no boy seemed interested in me. I was surprised that I had a couple of dates during that time.

When I worked at WBKB, I had a crush on one of the engineers, Chuck (don't recall his last name). He lived in Skokie (called Niles Center then), and he started driving me home after work at night since I lived on Sunnyside Avenue in Chicago, which was on the way to Niles Center (later named Skokie). We began making out a little bit on those drives. He was married, and they had just had twin boys, so it was kind of a shock that I would be involved in that type of situation. I was around eighteen or nineteen; an age I later realized was a little late to begin being interested in the opposite sex. The whole Chuck thing ended when I left WBKB to go to the Milwaukee station WTMJ.

There I met another engineer, Nick, who began taking me out to dinner, and we began seeing each other regularly. He wasn't particularly good-looking; in fact, he was a little overweight and slightly bald, but he was the first man with whom I ever got intimate. Looks didn't matter to me. I admired only men that were smart and knew a lot about everything. Nick was that kind of person, but it all ended when I took the job in Cincinnati at the Taft-owned station, WKRC-TV.

Here's the full story of Al and me. His full name was Albert Jack Litwin (known as AJ or Captain Al). I met him through his father, Sam Litwin. I was in Florida on vacation, staying at a hotel with a friend of my mother. I had been working in Milwaukee at WTMJ-TV but was about to move to Cincinnati to their new television station, WKRC-TV, and I decided to go on the Florida trip before I reported

*This is when I went to Florida with one of my mother's friends. That's where I met Sam Litwin, who fixed me up with his son Al.*

*Here I am in the ocean on my Florida trip.*

*A close-up of me in Florida*

to Cincinnati.

At the hotel in Florida, a very nice, white-haired gentleman used to hang out there. I don't remember why. He was almost a professional bridge player, and I think that's why he visited so often. I began talking to him while I was there, but when I was about to leave, he asked me if I would give him my name and phone number for his son, who was in the process of moving from Washington DC, to Chicago. Al had been working with the Securities and Exchange Commission in Washington, but he, at his own request, had asked for a transfer to their Chicago office. He liked Chicago, and although he was born and raised in Detroit, he had gone to graduate school at Northwestern in Evanston and wanted to settle there. At first, I said I wasn't interested, but Al's father wouldn't quit, so I finally said okay. I went back to Chicago, and before I left for Cincinnati, I received a call from Al Litwin.

He had free tickets to the Goodman Theater where his cousin Dave

Litwin (Wynne) was in a play. It was only Wednesday night, so he had decided to stop his father's bugging him and called me.

I was 5'8" tall, and I didn't know how tall Al was so I wore flat shoes. When the doorbell rang, and I buzzed him in, I didn't know what to expect as he climbed to the third floor of our apartment building. When he finally made it to the top step, I saw him for the first time. He was tall enough and very nice looking. He came in and met my parents, and then we drove off to the Goodman. I don't remember the play, but it was good. On the way back home, Al stopped at a street vendor's stand and got some kind of sandwich. He asked me if I'd like one, and I said, "No." Eating from a street stand at 11:00 p.m. seemed quite chancy, but that was Al.

That's dad's cousin Dave. He changed his name from Litwin to Wynne. He was Aunt Faye's son. This picture shows one of his dramatic poses. He was going to be an actor.

I guess he thought I wasn't too bad, so after a couple of weeks, he called me for another date. Thus, we began going out, doubling with friends and getting to know each other. At first, I didn't like him because he seemed very "bossy" and was a "take charge" person.

One of our early dates was dinner at Riccardo's and was one of the most memorable I ever had. Al and I never stopped talking even as we ate. We laughed and questioned each other about our current lives and backgrounds. The freshness of his smile, the strength and beauty of his hands, and the kindness in his eyes captivated me. Of course, this is where he tried out his "famous" spoon trick where he placed a teaspoon across the top of a glass and hit the end of it, and it was supposed to land in the glass but ended up flying across the room and landed on someone else's table!

Al bounced around quite a bit. In Detroit, he received his bachelor's degree in accounting at Wayne State (formerly called the College of the City of Detroit). He then worked for the Security and Exchange Commission (SEC) in Washington DC, where he shared an apartment with his cousin Dave Gruber in the Rock Creek Park area and attended law school. He was a born teacher and moved to Chicago when he got a fellowship at Northwestern University where he taught in the business school.

Al was in the Army Reserves. When WW2 began, he left law school to join the army where he received the rank of lieutenant. He eventually became a captain, using his CPA knowledge to help in the planning of the D-Day invasion, working at the Allies HQ in London with Eisenhower. (If he had waited for the draft, he would not have entered with the lieutenant rank). He went to England and was there during the blitz. He even slept through a bomb that destroyed the building across the street from the hotel where he was staying! He mostly stayed in London, but he also traveled to Wales and Scotland. He had a serious girlfriend while there.

When the war ended, he could have gone back to Washington, but he loved Chicago so much he transferred from the SEC in Washington to Chicago's SEC. That's when I met his father Sam in Florida.

Al knew so much. There was no question I could ask him that he couldn't answer—literature, music, foreign affairs or politics. He loved my curiosity.

Al was a generous and inspiring person. He had a great spirit and helpfulness and a special competence. Orderliness in thinking put everything in its correct place. He had a brilliant mind and was a fabulous listener. He adored talking with strangers, to learn about their lives and to offer assistance when he could. I remember him for his gentleness whether toward another person or a tiny spider. Whenever he would spot an insect in the house, he would find a way to capture it without hurting it and deposit it outdoors. I admired his kindness and patience with others, even those I might not have shown patience. Our attraction was strong and endured long into our marriage. I could say in all honesty that we never had a serious fight.

One day, he told me he was leaving the SEC to go into private practice as a CPA. He took a space in an office at Dearborn and Clark.

He printed stationery and cards, got a typewriter, phone/number, and joined the Covenant Club—a private Jewish club on Monroe—and began building his practice. He met many business people through his membership and acquired his first client, Fred Ex Motors.

*Al at five or six years old*

Al found out that I was a dynamic typist, and I soon found myself after work going to his little office and typing tax returns and financial statements as his business grew. We began serious dating for almost two years. Sharing nights in the downtown office, we began being intimate and going away on weekend trips. I always pretended I was visiting girlfriends in different cities. I remember one trip to Green Bay, Wisconsin, where we were surprised to bump into two of Al's friends, a little embarrassing because in those days, couples didn't "shack up" like they do now.

When he was at Wayne State University, he could take any elective, so, just for fun, he took a cooking class. It was so unusual that someone took a photo of him, and it made the local papers. "Albert Litwin sifting flour for muffins," it says on the picture.

Albert Litwin sifting flour for muffins.

*My darling Al*

*Al in pants they used to call knickers, the boys' fashion in those days*

*Al as a Boy Scout*

We had a chef's hat, but I think I gave it to one of the kids.

Al loved reading, the outdoors, was very smart, and had a great sense of humor, although he was one of the most unhandy men I had ever met. He loved traveling and trying new restaurants and different experiences. He loved everything that I loved. As he had been an Eagle Scout in the Boy Scouts, he maintained those values. It was during that time, I think, that we fell in love.

We dated over two years, in spite of my various aunts asking about where this friendship was going. After I met Al, there never was anyone else in my life. That was in the late 1940s.

One night, we were having dinner at a new restaurant in

*Al in a sailor suit*　　　　　　　　　　*Al, the businessman*

Lincolnwood when we began talking about getting married. The next thing I knew, I had accepted Al's proposal. I received a beautiful ring and announced our engagement to everyone. Al was not only smart, good-looking, and a hard worker; he also was compassionate, generous, and loving.

We set a wedding date for April 1, 1951 (April Fools' Day) because the tax filing deadline was March 15 back then. We figured April 1 would allow us to relax and enjoy our wedding and honeymoon. As it turned out, the IRS changed the deadline in 1954 to April 15, and we were able to celebrate our anniversary on the date only two times!

When I became engaged to Al, I didn't care about making any wedding plans, but my family did. Therefore, at their urging, we did have a somewhat large wedding. Afterward, I realized that, in my case, the wedding was more for my parents and their friends.

*Al and me*

Among the plans was buying a white wedding dress, so, to add to the excitement, I purchased a beautiful white dress at Saks Fifth Avenue on Michigan Avenue. They didn't have my exact size and were going to have to send it to me. As we got closer to the wedding date, my dress still had not arrived. A few days before the wedding, I found out that Saks had sent it to Texas, and we couldn't get it back in time. April Fools! What to do? My Aunt Sarah came to the rescue. She borrowed a beautiful white wedding gown from one of her daughters-in-law that fortunately was my size. With a little fixing up, it was perfect.

We had a beautiful wedding at Anshe Emet Temple, (where I had worked help-ing their great rabbi, Solomon Goldman, with

*Al & Dorothy's wedding*

*Our wedding*

his book). Officiating was Rabbi Goldman, and following the ceremony, we continued the celebration with a dinner-dance with over
one hundred people at the Orrington Hotel in Evanston. I picked the

Orrington because I loved their creamed spinach. What a silly reason to pick a restaurant, but the food was delicious. (Many years later, my nephew Norman married Maria at the same hotel, and Sandy had his Northwestern graduation there.)

I thought it was the best wedding ever, but Al's Aunt Fay complained later that she was unhappy because her son Jack had sat with his friends instead of with her. My parent's friends, the Balas, were there, and Louie Balas played the harmonica with the orchestra.

After the party, we drove to a hotel across from the Museum of Science and Industry on the South Side and spent quite a bit of time opening wedding envelopes, learning from Al how to endorse checks properly, and observing that he liked the toilet paper to roll down from the top, and other important stuff. Next day, we started driving to Miami Beach. In Marietta, Georgia, we made a pact that we would never go to bed angry at each other.

When we got to Miami, it rained non-stop. After a few days, we decided to leave Miami, drive south until we saw sunshine. That was in Key West where we decided to park the car and board a small plane to Cuba. In Havana, the weather was beautiful. (More on this in the Travel chapter)

# New House Surprise

During dinner that night in Lincolnwood, after Al had proposed, he sprang the news that he had just bought us a house. When I think back on it, one doesn't buy something as important as a house so casually. It's usually a couple's decision, but I didn't care. I thought it was wonderful. The house had four bedrooms and a bathroom on the second floor, and another bathroom in the basement. It had a big front porch the entire width of the house with an old-fashioned swing. The living room, fully carpeted, also ran the width of the house. I was delighted. The house had an attic with 8-foot ceilings, and after we married and returned from our honeymoon, Al used it for his office.

*New house surprise*

*Here's Al, possibly with Jim.*

The new house was located at 2928 Wilson Avenue in the Ravenswood Manor neighborhood in Chicago. It was a lovely neighborhood of old houses and tree-lined streets.

Within the year, I was pregnant with my first born, James Matthew, who arrived on January 8, 1952, a beautiful baby. Within seventeen months, I had my second son, Douglas Allen, (June 6, 1953), another beautiful baby. I used to

*Here we are at some kind of a party or wedding.*

remember June 6 was D-Day, but it was also Doug Day. At that time, Al used one of the four bedrooms as an office, and I spent many days in that office typing tax returns and financial statements with one of the babies in a "jump seat" next to me; Al bought the house because he had gotten a bargain.

Later, we learned that he had bought the house cheap because the next-door neighbor was a "nut." The previous owners had put her on a peace bond and sold the house at a loss because they wanted to get away from her. She wouldn't allow anyone to walk on her property, and when we went to fix the fence between our houses, she stood there swinging a hammer if the workman tried to reach over to hammer in a nail. She lived with her bachelor brother and kept pigeons in her house. She made our lives miserable.

After living there for two or three years, we decided to sell the house and move. We went house hunting with real estate agents to find another home, hopefully in the suburbs. I loved Highland Park where my Aunt Miriam and Uncle Hy lived, but taxes and prices were way beyond our means.

After trudging around looking for a house we could afford, we decided to build. I began looking at vacant lots. We decided that we could afford, house and lot, no more than $32,000. One day, I found a lot 66 feet wide by 132 feet deep in Skokie.

It was the tax season, and when I called Al to tell him about it, he said I should buy it. (When it rained, a small creek ran through the property, and, while we didn't think much of it then, this was probably the source of our basement flooding for many years, despite a lot of money spent on waterproofing.)

We bought the lot for $6,000 and began making plans to build our dream house. When we began working with a young architect, we soon realized that our "dream" house would break the budget, so we cut out a number of things. Instead of a center colonial entrance across the width of the lot, we turned the house around so the entrance was on the south side. We still had four bedrooms and a bathroom on the second floor, and we added a powder room on the first floor and one in the basement.

I remember one day when I drove to Skokie with Jim and Doug to see how the construction was coming along, Doug was still taking a bottle. He disappeared in the house, and when I found him, he was inside one of the uninstalled kitchen cabinets drinking his bottle; he had helped himself to it from my bag.

It took about nine months to build the house, and when it was ready, a couple of neighborhood children somehow managed to get in and splash paint on the walls and floors, so we had to delay our move-in date while the damage was being repaired.

We finally moved in with very little furniture, mostly hand-me-downs, but we managed. We were very, very happy in our new house, except I had two miscarriages before Sandy was born in 1956, one with twin boys and the other with a girl.

On December 27, 1956, I had my third son, Sanders Robert (Sandy), named after Al's father Sam. He wasn't too happy about his nickname, Sandy, because he said it was a girl's name, so, years later when he was on the air in radio, he became known as Bob Sanders. He called himself Sandy Shore at another station. Marty came along in September 1963.

We put our Chicago house on the market, asking $18,000 and sold it. Our Skokie address was 9627 N. Keeler Avenue, and our new phone number was ORchard 4-5221. We didn't use area codes then, but later it was 312 for all of Chicago and the suburbs. Later, our area code changed to 708, then to 847. It kept changing as more and more people moved to the suburbs.

We got to know our neighbors, the town, where to shop, schools and more. We absolutely loved it. Al was busy building up his CPA practice, and eventually we furnished the house, landscaped, built a garage, a room addition, and added air conditioning. Al was one of the un-handiest men I knew. But he was also one of the greatest guys you could imagine. The whole family looked to him for advice and help.

❧——❧

I now have four grown sons and six grandchildren. If the twin boys and the girl had survived, we would have had a grown daughter, probably with kids of her own, and a hockey team—SIX grown sons—a total of seven children. But I don't dwell on those things. It might have been possible to save the girl, even at six months, but with the cord strangulation, she was already gone. I don't know what they do with those fetuses. I never asked and I don't want to know. The twin boys would have been a first as we didn't have twins on either side of the family.

When Al was using the basement for his office, we called Niles North High School and asked for their best accounting students. They sent a boy and a girl. The boy worked for him, and later we tried the girl. Her name was Nancy Johnston, and she started working for Al when she was a junior and continued after graduation. She said she didn't want to go to college, but a year later, Al convinced her to go to Oakton Community College, a two-year school, and when she graduated, she was honored at a state of Illinois dinner as one of the twelve outstanding students in the whole state. Of course, Al paid all her tuition and expenses. A few years later, Nancy became a CPA with one of the highest test scores, and when Al retired, Nancy took over his practice.

# *Raising Four Sons*

*My four sons*

Before Marty came along, I remember taking the three boys to Kiddieland (although it was actually called Fun Fair at the time), and I had just found out that I was pregnant. I thought, God, I don't need this. I can't believe it. I don't need another baby. I have three of them already. But what am I going to do?

Marty was a wonderful baby, easy delivery, no problem in pregnancy. He was a big baby too—nine pounds fourteen ounces, just shy of ten pounds. I had stopped smoking during pregnancy. I always smoked cigarettes with the other pregnancies, and all three babies weighed about seven-and-a-half pounds, but I believe Marty was a big baby because I had stopped smoking.

Quitting smoking was one of the hardest things I have ever done—like trying to stop eating. I was a smoker and Al was not, but he never asked me to stop. Every winter, I would come down with bronchitis due to my smoking. I would cough, but it was more like barking. I remember one night I couldn't lie down. I was sitting on the couch in the living room, smoking, coughing and sipping hot drinks, and even some wine because I had heard that it was good for a cough but nothing helped.

I told myself I had to stop smoking. And I did, but it had been a serious addiction, a pack-a-day habit. I remember telling all of my children that I was going to be miserable and mean until I broke this bad habit. I said, "Remember this, and don't ever pick up a cigarette or a cigar. You'll get hooked on it." And I was really addicted. I finally made it after two weeks of not smoking and that was fifty-three years ago. I guess my sons might have tried smoking in college, but none of them smokes now.

About my sons: All are very, very smart, tall, good-looking, and very thoughtful, sensitive, and well liked by everybody. All of them took piano lessons and learned to read music. They loved books—Jim was into science fiction, Doug loved war stories, Sandy preferred sports, and Marty liked history. When they were in junior high, they had to learn to play an instrument or sing in the choir, whether they liked it or not. Marty didn't like it, but later on in junior high, he decided to play the trumpet. Sandy, with the help of the music teacher, chose the trombone. His music teacher actually picked that instrument for Sandy because he had the longest arms.

**Jim**, the oldest, always loved singing, has a wonderful baritone voice, and has always joined choirs whenever possible. In high school, in addition to being in the choir, he also wanted to learn to play the violin. His teacher, Thelma Wilcox, taught him as a freshman, and he joined the high school orchestra. He also was involved in theater. He played a guard in *Kismet* and won the starring role of Curly in the musical *Oklahoma*. In addition to musicals, he played Helen Keller's father, Capt. Keller, the male lead, in *The Miracle Worker*. He also played the male lead in *Mame*, a character named Beauregard Jackson

Pickett Burnside III.

When he graduated from Niles North High School, he couldn't wait to get away from home, or at least that's what he said. Northwestern had accepted him, but he decided to go with his friends to the University of Illinois in Champaign. He wasn't happy down there, and before he finished his first semester, he came home. After doing nothing for a while, he suddenly discovered Columbia College in downtown Chicago. How he ever discovered this place, I don't know. Its location was in an old building right on Lake Shore Drive. In a way, it was a "trade" school for the arts. Jim majored in film and loved it. He worked as a film editor at Coronet Films, making educational films, and then opened his own film business, calling it Anything Film.

When he graduated with a bachelor's degree from Columbia College, he decided to go to Northwestern University's Graduate School of Management (where Doug had graduated in 1976). Later it became the Kellogg School of Management. In 1979 after two years, and with an MBA, he received offers for positions all over the United States.

He accepted a job at Coors in Golden, Colorado. He was married to Sue Giffin, whom he had met through her PR job, and who did catering in Colorado and eventually PR with the leading advertising/public relations firm in Denver. They later moved to the Hartford, Connecticut, area where he worked for Heublein.

Jim also lived twice in San Francisco, divorced Sue, dated and married Maureen McGarrity, which turned out to be a very short marriage. He then met Doris Schlesinger through their mutual friends, Ruth and Mike Elbaum.

They were married August 16, 1987, at the "purple" Hyatt hotel in Lincolnwood. A few days before, Chicago had the worst rainstorm in history, and the lower level of the hotel flooded—where the ceremony was to take place. But the maintenance staff got it all cleaned up just in time. It was a beautiful ceremony, but the rabbi, as part of the ceremony, told a long, long story using numerology as it related to Jim and Doris. The hotel was fine for the ceremony, but when they were taking wedding pictures, I remember they asked me to take off my shoes in order to make a better picture, but the carpeting was soaking wet and so were my feet for the rest of the night. Doug had flown in for the wedding but made it only to St. Louis because O'Hare airport flooded, and no one could get in, so he returned to San Francisco. Sandy, en route from Florida, met with a delay in Atlanta and wound up spending the night at the airport. He got a flight the next morning and made it to the wedding. He never lets Doug forget about that.

Doris and Jim had three children: Brian Hans, Matthew Samuel, and Laura Emily. Jim got very high-paying jobs in marketing and bought a house in Buffalo Grove, IL. He began a new business, My Life Story, where he scanned pictures, documents, and memorabilia for customers and made videos from them. It was a wonderful idea, but because he would go to customer's house to scan everything, he found out that people would become nostalgic about their pictures and begin reminiscing, which took a lot of time, more than he had thought. It turned out that he had spent so much time on these house calls that the value of his time diminished to a point that his hourly rate was too low.

**Doug** was a good baby and easy to bring up. When he was about eight, he started piano lessons, and later when he was in fifth grade, he began playing the clarinet. He was in the orchestra and band, very musically gifted. He could sit down on the piano bench and start pecking out tunes when he was only about four years old. He played in the symphonic and marching bands at the University of Illinois where he got his undergraduate degree in business. He was the first to go to Northwestern and get his MM (later called a MBA). Right out of business school, he landed a marketing job at Brown & Williamson Tobacco and moved to Louisville. Then he got a job with a wine company in San Francisco in 1978. He's been there ever since. He bought a wonderful Victorian house that had been built in 1883 in the Noe Valley neighborhood; he paid $181,000. Al didn't think he should pay that much. When he finally sold it after thirty-four years of living there, he got $3,400,000! Actually, he now lives on a 55-foot, three-bedroom, three-bathroom, yacht in Sausalito harbor. He's very active with his band, The San Francisco Lesbian/Gay Freedom Band, and still plays clarinet and saxophone, along with percussion, when the band marches. He is also active with the international Gay Games organization, and with this group, he has traveled to Africa, Germany,

Australia, the UK, France, Netherlands and other countries around the world.

**Sandy** is the tallest son at almost 6'5", even though I smoked through his pregnancy. (Jim wondered if he might have been 7' tall if I hadn't smoked!) Sandy saw a coupon for an exercise program somewhere, saved some money, and sent away in hopes it would make him grow taller. It didn't work. He wore a size 15 shoe when he was in high school. They didn't have big and tall stores at that time, but there was one in Boston, the only one in the United States. We ordered new gym shoes, size 15. They finally came so he could wear them in gym class, although when he went to his locker, he found that somebody had stolen them. Now who would want a size 15 shoe? I mean, how many kids have feet that size? Anyway, we had to order another pair for him. Sandy played the trombone in seventh and eighth grade at Old Orchard Junior High. He did continue into his freshman year in high school but fractured his wrist during basketball tryouts that year, ending his trombone career. But when Vice-President Hubert Humphrey visited the junior high school, Sandy was in the band that played at that momentous occasion. He received his B.A. in Broadcast Communications from the University of Tulsa (1978) and, many years later, got his Masters in Communications from Northwestern (2002). He worked at radio stations for twelve years, from 1975 to 1987, starting at stations in Tulsa when he was in college. He moved on to stations in Coffeyville, KS; Davenport, IA; Cocoa Beach, FL (where he covered NASA space shuttle launches, including his award-winning coverage of the space shuttle Challenger explosion in January 1986 which he witnessed first hand while on the air broadcasting the launch); and Columbia, SC. He made his move into PR at the University of South Carolina and then worked at Centre East, handling many different things, including making the pre-show announcements ("no flash photography").

**Marty** was a very good baby, a big baby. He married Karin Fitzpatrick in 1995, and they have two great kids, Emily and Ben. They bought a house in Morton Grove and then moved to Algonquin as the kids starting getting bigger. Marty was a track and football star in high school and got scholarships to college until he injured his knees. Then he transferred to the University of Wisconsin where he got his degree. He started WAITRE D' DELIVERIES, a restaurant delivery service, which became a family business that we sold later. (More on this in the chapter on WAITRE D')

ᴄᴣ—ᴄᴣ

All four boys attended Highland School, which was walking distance from home. I was active in the PTA and was a room mother. When the Old Orchard Theater opened, I asked

*Me in my PTA days*

the owner if we could hold a fundraiser there for the PTA by showing a movie. He said yes and with just a small amount of promotion, we became swamped with attendees, who were eager to see what the new theater looked like inside. There were so many cars on Skokie Boulevard, trying to get in that the police had to come in to direct traffic.

In addition to ticket sales, we also operated the candy counter. "I remember that," says Jim. "Besides the fact that it was cool that my mother had rented a movie theater, we got candy and things and sold them at a concession stand."

Yes, we had to get our own supplies. Grocery stores would donate boxes of candy. There was also a place called the Mostow Company, which was a warehouse-type place that sold all kinds of things at discounted prices. They didn't donate that candy, but we used the concession counter to sell our own candy. We ended up making a lot of money.

I remember that the film was *The Long, Long Trailer*, starring Lucille Ball and Desi Arnaz. Many PTA mothers volunteered as

ushers, concession stand operators, and ticket takers. Jim and Doug also helped. We operated the box office. It was incredible. At the end of the day, I had an empty cigar box and a moneybag for the money. There was so much cash that it began to overflow. I stuffed my pockets until I could get another container.

That night, I took the overflowing containers to the bank to deposit it as a "night drop." I wasn't sure how to do that. I remember putting the money on the passenger seat and covering it with my coat so no one could see it, and then I deposited it.

That event was a huge success. The theater never rented it out again. They did not invite us back.

One day, when Jim was a junior high student, a tornado hit the school and took part of the roof off the building. In fact, I was driving the next day and saw part of the roof plastered against the fence around the cemetery a couple of blocks away. Jim said that the teacher was the first to run out the door. Fortunately, no one was hurt.

# Jim's Stories from Childhood

## Having the fun house on the block

Many people who grew up in the neighborhood told me that the Litwin house was always the fun place to go as we were always doing something wacky. Some of this apparently was because they weren't allowed to do those things in their houses, and some because we were very creative with our imagination in the games we played. I have also heard from them that my Mom often came up with unique and fun activities for us to do. I think this creativity may have been born out a desire to keep us occupied so we wouldn't fight or get into other trouble. Somehow we still managed to do so!

## Spray painting on side of house

I'm not sure who did this, (probably Doug or I), but one of us spray painted the letters "B" and "O" on the bricks on the side of the house that the garage eventually covered (where there was a water faucet). This was about as bad a swear word as our little minds could think of at the time as it stood for "Body Odor," and we thought it was funny. This was in blue paint in letters probably four feet high each and very visible to cars driving south on Keeler Avenue. Fortunately, when we built the garage, it completely covered the letters. (Maybe that's why the garage was built?) I assume that if you went into the garage today, you could still see those letters, faded though they might be. That would be alongside the pulleys on the ceiling joists where Dave Blake and I built a slot car track that we could raise on ropes to the ceiling so the cars could park there.

## Hose fighting in the house

We used to have epic water fights outside with squirt guns. But one time, I decided to bring some real firepower to bear and used the spray gun hooked up to the garden hose. This was too much for my brothers who fled into the house. In becoming carried way with my success, apparently I followed them into the house with the hose and continued spraying! As you can imagine, this was quite a mess to clean up…

## Throwing bat at Doug

Doug and I had one of our many, many fights. We were out in the corner of the backyard, playing baseball, and Doug did something to make me really mad and then ran away diagonally across the yard. When he was almost all the way across the yard, my anger got the better of me, and I threw the baseball bat at him. I watched it fly end over end for dozens of feet until it hit him squarely in the back of the head (a feat of throwing accuracy I'm sure I could not replicate again, even now as an adult). Doug's head started bleeding, and my mother took him to the hospital emergency room where he got a butterfly bandage. I think my father punished me with the dreaded "belt"!

Doug added, "It was the neighbor Bernie Kahn that helped drive us to Evanston Hospital, me with a bloody towel on my head. Once there in the emergency room, I overheard the doctors talking about putting stitches in my head. When the doctor came over to examine my head again, I let him know that I didn't want anyone stitching up my head, by throwing up all over him. That's when they went to Plan B and put a butterfly bandage on my head."

## Shaving kid's head

With four sons, taking us all for haircuts was a major chore for my mother (and expensive, to boot). Therefore, my mother bought an electric clipper set so she could do the haircuts at home. Doug and I decided to play barber with a little neighbor boy named Bobby (I think). In any case, we sat him down, put the apron thing around him, and proceeded to use the clippers to shave a stripe down the center of his head. Kind of a reverse Mohawk! I think we all thought we had done a great job and sat around admiring our work. Even Bobby liked it. Until he got home. Not sure what punishment we got for that, but Bobby and his family moved out of the neighborhood shortly after that. Don't know if the haircut incident had anything to do with that move, but it didn't help.

**Working for the ice cream bike company**

There wasn't a lot of work available for young teenagers, but somehow Doug and I (or maybe just I) got hired to ride bikes with coolers on them from a location on Howard Street over to the beaches in Rogers Park to sell ice cream. Someone dropped us off at the ice cream bike company, and the owner told us what to sell, which beaches to go to, and we left. But these bikes were pretty rickety, and before we made it to the beach, they fell apart. (Maybe the chain came off?) Somehow we were able to get to a phone booth and call for help, and someone (maybe our mom) came and got us. We never made it to the beach! And that was the end of our ice cream career.

**Getting Hanukkah gifts the fun way**

We received presents for each night of Hanukkah, and they would get progressively bigger each night. To make it more fun, our parents would hide the presents and give us hot, warm, or cold clues when we tried to find them. That made it extra special. (This is a tradition that I have kept with my kids to this day.) One morning when we were very young, we woke up to find a red ribbon attached to the stair railing. We followed this all the way downstairs, through the family room to the basement stairs and down to the basement. When we got down there, we found the ribbon attached to a very cool Lionel train set that was running around a track! It was the best present ever delivered in the most creative way possible. I also remember that, after the train cars broke at some point, we had just as much fun pushing the wheels around the tracks in kind of our own version of Hot Wheels. We were very creative in how we played with our toys. Give us a large empty box from a large appliance, and we have a spaceship or a castle.

## Taking trips to Wilmette Beach

For many years, we had passes to Wilmette Beach, and on nice days in the summer, we would drive over there in the station wagon for a day of swimming and sand castle building. These trips marked one of the family traditions that our father started because you could see the water when you made one of the last turns on Lake Avenue on the way there. He would always say, "The first one to see the lake yell 'Yeah, lake!'" So we were distracted looking for the lake instead of fighting with each other. We would always come back covered in sand, so my parents built a downstairs bathroom with a shower stall in it for us to wash off so we wouldn't track sand into the upstairs part of the house.

## Experimenting with fire

I was a bit of pyro when I was a kid. (Maybe this fascination with fire was because of my experience in "The Explosion.") One time, I decided to experiment with matches. I lined up the match heads of about fifteen matches on the countertop in what we called the yellow bathroom. Then I lit one on the end and watched as they all lit in order, one after the other like a fuse. Unfortunately, the heat of the burning matches caused the Formica surface of the countertop to blister, and that damaged countertop remained that way for many years until we remodeled the bathrooms and replaced the countertops.

Another time, I was building model Estes rockets. I glued a fin onto the tube of the rocket and decided that if I applied some heat on the glue, it would dry faster. So I put a bare light bulb next to the fin to heat it up. It did dry faster, BUT since it was close to the laminate top of my desk, the heat also caused that surface to melt a little and blister. We moved that desk module to Sun City in Huntley, and to this day, you can still see the small area where I had damaged the desk!

Of course, we were fascinated with fireworks. Elliot Miller, one of our friends on Keeler Avenue, always seemed to have pop bottle rockets and firecrackers, which we LOVED when he shot them off in the street. Sometimes, we would lay a bottle rocket on its side in the street, and when we lit it, it would shoot up the street, leaving a long trail of sparks. Other times, we pretended that we were having a war and shot them back and forth at each other up and down the street.

We were always desperate to get our own fireworks. Elliot told us the secret was to go to a certain store in Chinatown and ask for Louie, but we never had a chance to try that out.

Years later, I was able to get some fireworks, including one called a "Zizz-Bang" which was a little saucer that would spin up in the air and then explode with a bang. The first time I lit one of these, it flew right into my face, even though I was standing far away. Fortunately, no damage, but the others watching this thought it was hilarious. Ask Neill Sachs!

## Turning the basement bathroom into a darkroom

In later years, the downstairs bathroom was not used much. When I had started developing my own film and making prints at Columbia College, I turned that bathroom into a darkroom. I hung a red safe light in there so I could see what I was doing and used the sink to process the film. However, I needed a flat surface to put my enlarger on to make prints, so I took a piece of plywood and cut it to fit the shower stall. My mother got mad at me because I drilled holes in the metal walls of the shower stall to support the table.

## Experiencing a tornado

It was about May 1965, and I was in the seventh grade in social studies class. I was somewhat bored of the lecture and kept looking out the window at the rain. I noticed that the rain was getting stronger, and the winds were blowing.

Suddenly, the trees started swaying to one side, and that rather reminded me of newsreels of Florida hurricanes with the palm trees blowing to one side. The teacher didn't seem to notice any of this going on.

Then the rain really started blowing against the window so strongly that I couldn't see anything. It was like a wall of water hit the glass, and everything was white. There was a loud noise from outside, and everyone started heading for the door. I remember my teacher was the first one out!

We all huddled in the hallway against the lockers. I don't remember if the lights went out (I don't think so), but then it was over. I don't remember exactly what happened next, but eventually we learned that school was going to be let out early.

When we got outside, what we saw was amazing. Much of the roofing material had blown off and landed in the parking lot alongside the building. The flagpole had bent sideways! The yellow school bus in the circular driveway, waiting to take kids on a field trip, had a big dent in the roof where some of the roofing material had hit it. It reminded me of a big metal can with a dent on its side. Black tar paper from the roof covered many cars in the parking lot.

I'm not sure if I took a bus home or walked. But I remember that the air, which had been heavy and humid earlier, was now kind of cold and refreshingly dry.

This storm may not actually have been a tornado but straight-line winds called a microburst or a derecho, but meteorological science had not advanced that far back then. Whatever it was, it just affected the junior high and not the apartment building across the street or Sharp Corner School on the other side of the school. If it was a tornado, it just brushed the roof of my junior high and fortunately nothing else.

*Clean-up after the tornado*

I don't recall if there were holes in the roof after the incident. I didn't see any, but a lot of the roof had been blown off, so there could have been holes. I think some of the windows incurred damage. In the accompanying photos, it looks like work men on ladders were working on them.

## Pets

As can be expected in a house with four boys, we had a variety of pets over the years. We had the usual goldfish and turtles, but those didn't usually last very long. I always heard the story about how my father brought home a dog for us, but when he opened the car door in front of the Wilson Ave. house, the beast ran away and we never saw him! More longer-lasting pets included Tuffy, a black cat that supposedly one of us picked up by the tail and spun around; Snoopy, a beagle/ hound mix that loved to bark at squirrels through the front picture window and rip up the mail as it came through the slot next to the front door; and Tar, a black collie/German shepherd mix that we raised from a puppy. We loved them all!

> Marty added about Tar: I remember Tar used to climb one of the trees in our backyard. It was one of the trees in "stone city" that was at about a 45-degree angle, and he'd run up it like a ramp and sit there. I never saw another dog do something like that.
>
> Doug added about Tuffy: My recollection about Tuffy is that one day he just ran away from home. Maybe he got tired of being swung around by the tail. I think one of us decided to test out that phrase "There's not enough room in here to swing a cat!" As the story goes, a year or two after Tuffy ran away, one of us spotted him running around an alley with some other cats. When we tried to get him to come back inside the house, he wasn't the least bit interested. I'm not sure I blame him!

Sandy added about Tuffy: I admit I'm the one that swung him around by the tail (I was VERY young at the time). I guess I just wanted to see how "Tuff" he really was. By the way, I still don't like cats very much.

*The Litwins and Roths at Sue Roth's wedding in 1972 with Mother in the middle.*

# The Explosion

One of Al's oldest clients, Nate Nudelman, owner of 20th Century Plastic, always invited our family to all kinds of parties and events, whether at his home, at his plant or even at a resort. Once a year, or more, he would invite his key employees and us to business meetings at various resorts in the area. On Memorial Day weekend in 1959, he invited us to go to a dude ranch near Wild Rose, Wisconsin. It was not very far from Stevens Point. I didn't really want to go because Sandy was only a year and a half old, and with Jim and Doug, I felt it was just too much, but Al didn't want to go by himself, so I said okay because Nate had been so nice to invite us. We packed everybody up and took the trip. They had just opened up the Illinois Tollway, so we took it for the first time. It was cold and raining the whole way up there, rather miserable.

We finally got to our cabin at night. When we went in, it was very cold and smelled very musty. The boys came in with Al and me and the daughter of a friend of Nate. She was going to be a dancer; she was twelve years old, I think. The boys were all lying on the beds.

It was very cold in the room, and Al thought he'd light the space heater in the room, but he did not know how, so he called the manager. She came over and explained that they had just installed new carpeting that day, and in order to lay it, the workers had to disconnect the space heater. They had put it back but didn't light it, so she said she would do that for us.

Meanwhile, it was so musty in the room that I opened some of the windows. I heard her say, "I'm going to light it."

I said, "Don't light it." I don't know why I said that. I didn't know there was a problem, and there was no gas smell. There was just the musty odor.

She struck the match, and the stove blew up and her clothes caught on fire. Dad was standing over her and tried put out the fire on her clothes with his hands; that's why he burned his hands. I remember thinking, I will run to the bathroom and go into the bathtub or the shower, and I'll be okay. I remember running, and that's all I remember about that.

The next thing I knew, someone was helping me get outside where there were several people. They put me in a car. I didn't know where Al was. I didn't know where the kids were. I remember seeing a little farmhouse, but I was in and out of consciousness. The farmhouse was the Wild Rose Hospital where we were taken. I don't know if the kids were in there, but I remember hearing Sandy crying for his bottle, and because I was mostly unconscious, there was nothing I could do about it. That's how we spent the night. I don't remember pain, just going in and out of consciousness.

**STEVENS POINT DAILY JOURNAL**

Monday, June 1, 1959

## Four Hospitalized Here As Result Of Resort Explosion

Four persons, all members of a Skokie, Ill., family, are receiving treatment at St. Michael's Hospital for burns received in an explosion in a resort cabin near Montello Friday.

They are Albert J. Litwin, 40, his wife, Dorothy, 33, and their sons, James, seven, and Douglas, six. Discharged from the hospital Sunday were another son, Sanders, two, and a friend of the family, Carol Willow, 15, Chicago.

*Local newspaper article about the explosion*

I remember that I had bandages on, and they were stuck to my burnt skin. Then the following day, they said they were going to take us to the hospital in Stevens Point. The next thing I knew, I was in a vehicle. I remember the interior has pink silk or satin padding, and I remember thinking, What the heck is this vehicle? Later on, I found out that it was the vehicle the little town of Wild Rose used for an ambulance and a hearse.

Then I remember waking up and learning I was in a Catholic hospital in Stevens Point with crosses and nuns and everything around us. They were wonderful to us. Somehow, the story got in the paper that a Jewish family was in the hospital. I don't know how they got the Jewish part but they did. Then I think a rabbi came around. The nuns were very good to us. One of them brought a radio and plugged it in so I could listen to music. I was still in and out of consciousness.

My mother and father drove up from Skokie, and then my father took the three kids back home while my mother stayed and handled arrangements to fly Al and me back to Chicago. All I remember is that I was in a little private plane on a stretcher. My mother was in there, but there was no place for her to sit, so she sat on the floor of the plane and had to hold on to the edges of the seats when the plane took off and landed.

After we landed, our family doctor, Dr. Harry Powell, met us at a small field at O'Hare. An ambulance transferred us to Edgewater Hospital. I guess I was the worst injured. Al stayed less time.

My mother and father were living in our house because my father had lost his job. Their plan was to get their own place once he began working again.

About the night of the fire, Jim remembers that it was very late. He was seven years old at the time.

"I remember being in bed, half sleeping, when all of a sudden five-foot flames were shooting everywhere in the room. We ran to the screen door, but it was stuck and wouldn't open right away. Once I got outside, I was jumping up and down in pain and looking at my arms with black burnt skin all peeled and curled up. Everything else is kind of a blur. I remember in the hospital that I had bandages on, and when we got to the Stevens Point hospital, the bandages were stuck to my burnt skin. They had to inject liquid under the bandages to get them off, and it hurt a lot.

"So the same thing must have happened to Doug, and that's why his right finger was bent so badly. Sandy had a burn on his stomach, and I heard that he had been outside the cabin when the explosion happened. He was standing right by the door on the outside and something hit him, something flaming. I remember seeing flames all around because the room was filled with gas."

Yes, there was a propane tank right outside. I learned later that propane naturally has no odor, so they usually added a gas smell so that people would know it's a dangerous gas. They hadn't done that, however, and that was the point of our lawsuit later on. I don't know if we sued the resort or the gas supplier or what. I think the hospital did nothing wrong, but it was beyond their capability to handle all of us in this little tiny farmhouse.

The hospital in Stevens Point did the best they could for us. They had to give me plasma a lot. I guess one result of burns is that you lose a lot.

When I got back to Chicago, I was at Edgewater Hospital for two or three months. I had skin grafts. They kept taking me up to surgery to remove skin from an unburned area and use it for the grafts. They put grafts on my arms and legs, and even now, you can see the marks on my legs. I think there were ten different visits to the operating room.

I remember looking at my arms, but generally, I didn't want to see the burns. However, the reflecting lights in the surgery room were like mirrors, and I once saw my black face, all burnt. Then I looked at my arms and said I'd never barbecue chicken again because it looked like the times when Uncle Maury used to cook chicken. He always burned it really black and crumbly looking, ugly.

I shared the room with Al, and then he went home. He was a terrible patient. He never had been in the hospital, except when he was born, I guess. So he would walk around the halls without a bathrobe on, and the nurses would say, "Put a robe on," but he wouldn't do it. He was just not happy about being there but who was?

One time, a nurse was dressing my wounds when my father called to see how I was doing. I said, "Can I call you back because the nurse is just putting medicine on me." She used something like a silver nitrate that burned like hell, but it brought the skin together.

That was the last time I ever talked to my father because when he left work, he went to our house, sat in the living room on the couch, had a heart attack, and died. He was diabetic.

Jim, who was about seven, wrote, "I remember very clearly seeing him lying on the couch, and the paramedics were putting something some kind of wires into his throat. I guess they were trying to resuscitate him. We have a lot to be thankful for, Laverne and Maury and your mother and father for taking care of us."

I don't know how we would have coped without family. I once heard Dr. Oz, the heart surgeon, say, "You've got to have somebody there when they operate. You have to have someone with you that loves you and you love them because that helps. If there's no one there, the heart seems to know and wants not to go on unless someone's there to take care of you."

I couldn't go to my father's funeral because I was still bedridden in the hospital. Eventually, I came home. The fire had burned my hair, and the surgeons had chopped it all off, so it was really a mess. I couldn't drive or anything. Finally, I went to the beauty parlor where they cut off all the burnt hair, but eventually it all grew back. That was never a problem with me. I remember they said at the beauty parlor that I was such a mess.

In fact, I sustained the worst burns, even though Al had been standing right behind the manager. One of the daughters of another attendee, who was also in the cabin, had wanted to become a dancer, but her legs were badly burned, and no one thought she would ever dance again. She did recover, though and resumed dancing.

It was a long time before I would go on the Tollway again because it brought back all the memories. In fact, I couldn't sleep. That's when Valium first came out, and the doctors gave it to me to calm me down.

Meanwhile Al hired an attorney, and it seemed that he wasn't doing anything about our case. We'd call him, and he would get really mad and say, "Don't bug me. I'm taking care of it." It took a long time, but he finally sued and we finally got a settlement. Each of the boys got a settlement, which we used to set up bank accounts for them. I don't remember how much. We got something, but it wasn't all that much when we came right down to it.

After the explosion, Jim had emotional problems. When he went back to school—second grade—his teacher called and told me that every time the janitor burned trash, Jim would start pacing the room, very upset. The school psychologist talked to me, and eventually, we took Jim to a private child psychologist. We went to his home in Evanston. It was hard to get him to open up, but the psychologist was just breaking through and getting Jim to talk when we learned that the doctor had suddenly died of a heart attack. (Sandy developed a comeback when Jim would criticize him, "At least I didn't kill my psychologist.")

We found a psychiatrist, this one in Winnetka, and Jim remembers that the house next door had trains kids could ride on in his backyard, and Jim was more interested in the trains than seeing the doctor. Plus, to Jim, it seemed that all they did in session was play games. But that's what they do, and eventually, kids start talking. Jim was always a high-strung child.

I remember that psychiatrist's house. Usually, gentile homes were always so neat and quiet. And our house was always in uproar and a mess. And now I have a house that doesn't get dirty hardly at all. It's very neat and quiet.

Al couldn't go to work at his office downtown on Randolph near Wells. I remember he asked our neighbor Ray Friedlander, who was in the same building, to pick up Al's mail, and sometimes he would and sometimes he wouldn't. It was very frustrating. That's how Al got his mail and occasionally a check. I don't know what happened to his clients. We didn't lose anybody, but he didn't have Nancy at that point. He didn't have anybody, really. I don't know how we handled it.

Doug's finger was permanently bent with scar tissue to where he couldn't open it. The doctor told me that when Doug grew into his forties, he would still have the finger of a six-year-old unless he had surgery. Because it had to grow with the rest of his hand, we decided Doug would undergo surgery.

It was the tax season. I was going to see Dr. Koch, a hand specialist who didn't operate on anything above the wrist. I went to meet him with Doug, and once, as were driving downtown, Doug was looking at all the high-rise buildings along Lake Shore Drive. And he said, "I'm going to be a musician, and I'm going to live in one of those buildings." Well, those two things don't normally go together. If you are a musician, you don't have enough money to live in those buildings.

Doug's remembers that he "wanted to work at McDonald's and live in one of those tall buildings. That never happened, but Jim actually managed to live out my dream. He had a job at a marketing agency where McDonald's was his primary client. At that time, he lived in a high-rise on Lake Shore Drive. Dreams do come true, although sometimes for a different brother!"

We met Dr. Koch, and he said, "Hi, how do you do?" He was kind of a gruff old guy, and his hand was shaking. I said to myself, *his hands are shaking. How is he going to operate on my child?* They said that when he gets in the operating room and picks up a scalpel, his hands are steady as a rock. Dr. Koch was so experienced that he wrote the book on hand surgery that other doctors used during their training. He did operate on Doug and mostly straightened out his finger. It's still kind of thick, and he still has a scar there, but it's normal and it grew. Doug, always very musical, still plays the clarinet as well as other instrument. He truly is a dedicated musician.

Doug recalls it like this:

"I remember running into the bathroom of the cabin to try and wash my hands to stop the burning. I also remember being in someone's station wagon driving away from the scene, looking back over my shoulder to see the walls of the cabin collapse. This was also the first time I was ever in an airplane, and I remember my Aunt Laverne being there to comfort me.

"The hospital experiences are somewhat of a blur, but I do remember being in court and sitting in the witness chair. During the lawsuit, I also remember people saying, "We're waiting for our ship to come in." I used to sit in the front window of the house staring at Keeler Avenue, hoping a big ship or boat would come down the street. Now I live on one! To this day, I won't light the pilot light of a gas appliance. I'll have someone else do it while I stand across the street."

# King of the Road

Al and I loved going on trips, especially car trips. But traveling with four boys was not fun. We would go on trips with them, and we'd be in the most terrific spots and say, "Look at this! Look at that!" They'd all be fighting in the backseat, so Al had a plastic Whiffle bat in the front seat, and he would reach back with the bat and threatened to use it if they didn't stop. "Hit 'em with the bat!" became a family saying. It was terrible traveling that way. The fights would get so bad that the car would sway from side to side!

We read an article about this new thing called motor homes. We got very interested and said that that would be the way to travel because the kids could play games, sleep or eat or do whatever they wanted to do. I guess technically you weren't supposed to walk around back while the vehicle was moving, but back then there were no seatbelts.

We decided to test the waters and rented a motor home from Mal Bellairs, a radio announcer on WBBM, whose home was in Winnetka. I remember the house, a big white house. We rented his motor home and took the first trip. We went down to St. Louis and parked in the parking lot of the ball field where a game was underway. The parking lot was full, but we got a spot there. (This was the old Busch Stadium where the Cardinals played).

We woke up the next morning, all alone in this huge parking lot with no cars there, just us. A couple of cars pulled in, and the people knocked on our door. "What is this?" they asked. "We'd like to come in and see what it is." They came in and looked around. In fact, we were having breakfast at the time, and Al invited their kids to join us for breakfast.

We loved the motor home. Traveling in it was just great. We could cook, sleep, and play games while we were on the road. We could stop in towns, buy groceries, and learn about the areas. I loved shopping in these little stores and seeing groceries that I had never heard of before.

In St. Louis, there was a fire station across from the big parking lot just outside the arena. The firemen came over and knocked on the door. They wanted to know about our motor home, so we took them on a tour. The whole idea fascinated them because, unlike a trailer, the motor home was fully powered. It was a home and a vehicle, an all-in-one unit built on a Ford chassis. The engine was between the two front seats.

We decided to buy one. Al did the research, flew to a factory in California, and purchased a 21-foot model called the Pace Arrow. He also signed up, became a dealer, formed a company, and named it "King of the Road." I think we paid $6,000 for the unit.

A motor home is a self-contained unit with sleeping accommodations for six and a galley-like kitchen with cabinets, stove, oven, refrigerator and dining table. It had a large heater and a bathroom with shower and toilet facilities. Our unit had its own generator in case we parked

*Pace Arrow Motor Home*

where there was no place to plug in for an overnight stay. We also had a 50-gallon gas tank, a water tank, and a holding tank for sewage. We had an eight-track player built into the dash, along with our radio, so we could play the song *King of the Road* when we participated in RV/ Camping shows.

After purchasing a motor home and becoming a dealer, Al flew back to Chicago, and the owners of the factory drove the motor home to us. It was their first motor home east of the Mississippi. Somehow, I remember that the door flew open once and bumped me in the head.

Our first trip was to the Indiana dunes with our niece Nancy and our boys. Once there, we had a great time rolling down the hilly sand dunes. On the way back to Chicago, the motor died. We pulled over, and the motor was smoking. I stood over the motor with the fire extinguisher in hand, and Al got out of the unit to try to find help. He had to climb over a fence, and, in doing so, lost his glasses. He saw a farmhouse in a field, and he got to where he could make a phone call. I think someone towed us back to Chicago.

The first big trip we took was to Florida. We began having mechanical problems right away, and when we got to Georgia, the head gasket blew. We were stuck in this little town called Unadilla, Georgia, for a few days while the Ford dealership fixed the engine. Being in a small southern town was a real education for the boys. I remember this one guy said when we invited his children to have breakfast with us, "You're eating with these Yankees?" They also ate grits for the very first time.

On another trip, we drove to Florida, and the motor home became stuck in the sand next to our hotel, but after someone pulled us out, we had a wonderful time. Driving back north, the weather turned cold, and our heater stopped working. We were all freezing, so we decided to stay overnight in a motel in Louisville, Kentucky. We checked in—it felt so good. We all took hot showers to warm up. Then Al went out to get us some food.

After we ate, we realized we had to get back into the motor home to get our clothes and other things, but our door lock had frozen, so we had to try to get it fixed the next morning. We got someone to help unfreeze the lock, and we continued on our way back to Chicago. I think we made that trip when the kids were on Christmas vacation.

We did rent our motor home out to somebody, and they had a problem with it, too. Everybody had a problem with it. We learned later on that it was underpowered; the engine was not big enough for the unit size. Ford Motor Company sent a representative to interview us. He sat at the kitchen table while we told him what had gone wrong. He took a million notes because he realized that that was why everyone had trouble with it. They should have given us the money for it. They didn't give us anything. I think we ended up selling it.

I remember when we started renting it. We exhibited at the International Amphitheater Camping Show. I put all new sheets on the beds and brand-new towels in the bathroom. People would go through it, and the first evening I went back there, somebody had taken all the sheets and the towels. Somehow stole them right out of the building.

How do they get out of the building with those things? We were in there all the time. Don't know how they did it. They must have put it under their clothing or something.

King of the Road business card

We came up with the name King of the Road for our business based on the popular Roger Miller song. All of us had business cards, even the boys.

To get people to come to our exhibit, we rented a display water barrel with what looked like a giant faucet with water coming out of it continuously from no apparent source. The faucet looked like it was just floating in thin air about six feet up. (There was a clear supply pipe in the center of the water stream that pumped the water back up to the faucet, but because it was clear, you couldn't see it.)

Many people found that attractive. Marty was still a very young kid. We had to close the unit down when it was time for him to take a nap with his bottle. It was an RV recreational vehicle show, but nobody had RVs at that point other than trailers. We had to explain that a motor home was a cross between a bus and a trailer.

I was looking at an RV place that opened a couple of years ago near here in Huntley. The motor homes right now are up to 45 feet long with sides that slide out when parked to give extra inside room. They are like very nice homes, and people live in them full time.

# Fine Arts Commission

When we first moved to Skokie, Jim started first grade at Highland School, which was a short walk from our home on Keeler Avenue. I joined the PTA and became involved in their activities. One time, they asked us to go to a local dance studio and learn how to do the hula dance. It turned out it was for a PTA fundraiser. We had to put dark makeup on our arms and legs, wear a luau outfit, and dance for two performances. After a matinee, I had to get some groceries before returning for an evening performance. So here I was, shopping in my Hawaiian outfit with all my makeup on.

I always joined choirs, and one was forming at the Skokie Park District. I joined immediately and began going to rehearsals. Al loved to sing, so he decided to join also. He had a beautiful deep baritone voice, but I think he didn't pass the audition. He really couldn't read music or hear very well. They say it has something to do with hearing ability, but I think it's also being able to tell if you're not matching the note. I would go "ahhhh" and sing a note, and he would go "ahhhh," and he'd be a halftone off. Al gave up, but he wondered aloud if singing lessons would help him. He never tried again.

The Skokie Park District sponsored the choir, and our conductor was Dave Politzer, a wonderful director who put together great programs. Dave was a clarinetist, sang professionally, directed the local high school choir, played with the Chicago Symphony Orchestra, and gave private lessons on the clarinet. When Doug became serious about his clarinet playing, Dave was his private teacher and helped him purchase his beloved Buffet clarinet, which he still uses.

The choir met at the Devonshire Park in Skokie. Our concerts were always a success, and everybody enjoyed the music. Dave planned a mixture of show tunes and classical pieces. We did a Bach piece, which was very complicated, kind of mathematical and challenging. We loved it. In the choir, I met Jane Meis, who would become my good friend, and a whole lot of other people. I sang alto at the time, and Jane was a soprano. I made many friends there.

One day, the superintendent of the park district said something to Dave that he did not like, so he went into the superintendent's office and reamed him out. He had a temper. So the park district fired him, and when we heard about that (this was the 60s), everybody walked out.

We then formed our own group with Dave as our conductor. We needed a place to rehearse and found space at the local bowling alley, and then the school district offered us space in the Jane Stenson School. When we grew to over sixty voices and needed a larger rehearsal hall, we received an offer of a larger space at Sharp Corner School. Under Dave's direction, we became very, very good and held many sold-out concerts.

Then Dave left us, and we formalized our group as the Skokie Valley Symphonic Choir. Jane and I became very involved in the operations of the choir. We had to hire a new conductor and an accompanist, and learn how to operate as a business. We got our 501(c)(3) not-for-profit incorporation standing from the Internal Revenue Service, opened a bank account, began charging dues, ordered music, and began paying for an accompanist.

Our first conductor after Dave left was Jim Wilson, who was great. Other conductors included Thelma Wilcox, the music teacher from Niles North; and Ken Eidson, who had sung with Homer and Jethro, a popular country duo in the 60s. We never knew if he was Homer or Jethro.

I remember when the first black family moved into town. Their last name was Fortune, and they had two sons who knew my boys and attended school with them. Their father was a chemist at one of the large pharmaceutical houses in Skokie, and their mother, Gwen Fortune, was a trained musician and a teacher in our schools. She joined our choir, and when we needed a new conductor, she offered, but the choir settled on someone else. She was very angry and accused us of racism, which it wasn't, but she had that chip on her shoulder. She had a great singing voice, and when she auditioned for a solo and wasn't selected, she was hurt and angry again.

One day, we learned that the village was setting up a fine arts commission similar to the start of the National Endowment for the Arts and the Illinois Arts Council. They wanted a representative from all of the arts groups in Skokie to join this commission. They already had representatives from the symphony orchestra, the art guild, a dance group, and a theater group, and they wanted our chorus to send someone to their first meeting. But nobody wanted to do it because nobody knew what the fine arts commission was. So I said I'll try it, and I became the representative for the choir to the Skokie Fine Arts Commission. And the state had just formed the Illinois Arts Council, so Skokie was very good about forming an arts commission. No other towns did that. Skokie was thinking far ahead of the other communities.

I began going to their meetings. At that time, the chairman of the commission was Seymour Einstein, an attorney, and later on Jerry Kaplan, another attorney who also played oboe in the Skokie Valley Symphony Orchestra. When I applied to Northeastern University, he was my sponsor.

I got more involved with the Fine Arts Commission. They didn't know what they should be doing, so I made some suggestions. I became familiar with all of the other organizations in the town and could see that they were all planning concerts, plays, or something. I thought there should be an arts calendar, showing all the things that were going on in the town; it would be good for all of them.

This was a village commission, so we were commissioners. I remember going to Al Rigoni, who at the time was the assistant village manager. He had just gotten his MBA. I told him that I wanted to put together an arts calendar that could go out with a village newsletter that went to all residents. The village had the newsletter typewritten and then printed at one of the firehouses where they had a little printing press. In order for us to get space in that newsletter, we had to volunteer to help with the folding of all the newsletters. There were seventy thousand newsletters! They came off the press, and we folded them three ways, so they could put the stamps on them.

And Rigoni said, "You can put the arts calendar in there, but don't make it look better than the rest of the newsletter." I remember thinking that wouldn't be much of a challenge because the newsletter didn't look THAT good! I began learning about how newspapers come together and what kind of printing there was by going into print shops and talking to people. I began putting together some articles that I wrote for the newsletter, and eventually we did our own arts newsletter. I put out the whole thing. The village gave the Fine Arts Commission a budget. It was small but

DOROTHY LITWIN, DIRECTOR of the Skokie fine arts commission was on hand this week when workers began installing the new light sculpture at the village green, Oakton and Lincoln, Skokie. As the sign announces, the sculpture by John David Mooney will be unveiled officially at a ceremony at 4 p.m. Sunday, Sept. 24.

*Fine Arts sign and me*

*Collage of Fine Arts articles*

LERNER-LIFE NEWSPAPERS, THURSDAY, NOVEMBER 21, 1974

WOMAN of the MONTH

## Skokie's fine arts dynamo was local television pioneer

Seymour Einstein, chairman of Skokie's Fine Arts Commission, presents a check for $700 to Mrs. Dorothy Litwin of the Skokie Valley Concert Choir, and for $1,000 to David Kantro of the Skokie Valley Orchestra

PIONEER PRESS | Suburban Century | Thursday, December 30, 1999 | 5

## Smith, Litwin, Radmacher had hands in shaping Skokie

it covered some things. I began thinking of programs, and we began putting them on at the library.

Jim put together one program for me. It was Tom Palazzolo, an independent filmmaker from the Art Institute. In addition, he helped me get a man from Yugoslavia, Selmer Matko, from the Zagreb Animation Studios, and Bob Edmonson from Columbia College. The program with Tom Palazzolo was very innovative. We had audience

*Skokie Library film flyer, designed by our neighbor, Armand Zucker*

members come up with ideas for a film and then help shoot the film in one session right in the library auditorium. Then in the next session, a couple of weeks later, we edited it again with the audience's suggestions. That was a great experience. Then a few weeks later, we premiered the finished film and hired a piano accompanist.

How did I go from being a member of the Skokie Fine Arts Commission to becoming the head of Centre East Performing Arts Center? Because, again, no one else wanted to do it.

It started with the programs. First, I would get a band. Before I got involved, an elderly man who owned a pizza place had put together a band of his friends or a union band. They would do a concert in the park every summer; it was a fairly bad concert. They were professional union musicians, but they weren't very good. Then I invited other bands to give concerts; Northwestern University brought out its premiere band, and other local schools also booked their bands. We began doing more concerts in the park.

What did I do? I saw that the Illinois Arts Council was going to have a granting program to pay executive directors of arts commissions one year at full salary, next year at three quarters, and then half, and then one quarter, and eventually the village would have to pick up the whole salary. I asked Al Rigoni about that, and he said, "Oh, I guess you could try it." I applied for it and we got it!

I named myself "executive director" and got a small salary. I had no idea what a salary should be. I found out that the crossing guards made $4.25 an hour, so that's what I put down for my salary. The village had a two-story brick building on Babb Street. They had been renting it to people who fell behind in their rent, and, when I got the grant, they had just kicked those people out.

I asked if we could use that building for the Skokie Arts Center, and they said okay. Before I moved in there, the village had their people paint the whole place and even tile the downstairs powder room. This was in 1975, and I had an office on the second floor. I had a donated desk that was very nice, and a desk chair and file cabinet. I gave one room to the Skokie Valley Symphony for their offices. The basement and the main floor of our building became a place for teaching art classes and a gallery where we featured their work. A Skokie community theater group sometimes held rehearsals there. The house is still there. Another time, I learned about a grant to support the cost of public art. As usual, I got involved and met John D. Mooney, a well-known light sculptor. At the point, I got funding for one of his light sculptures, which is now a permanent fixture on the Skokie Village Green between Village Hall and the library.

Back to the Babb Street building: I kept doing programs with the park district, the library, and the high schools. I even remember I got all three high schools in Niles Township to send their best singing groups for a concert or their best speakers for a debate. Because one high school did not know what the other high school was doing, I thought we'd mix it up like a talent show. Maybe we would mix up Niles East and West and North, so they would have to stay and watch the others.

Those were the kinds of things that I began working on, and I came to know people at the high schools—the superintendent, the teachers, and the library staff. Mary Radmacher was the chief librarian at the time, and then Carolyn Anthony got the job when Mary was diagnosed with breast cancer and had a mastectomy. Some complication with her lymph nodes caused her left arm to swell very badly all of the time, so she had to stop working.

We had a contest asking people to bring to the park district things that they had found. We then delivered the "found" items to an artist who turned them into sculptures. For example, someone found an old fender from a car or a bicycle wheel, and it became part of the sculpture which, when finished, was placed in front of the Babb Street house. This sculpture drew a lot of attention because it was really something quite different.

I completed my credit hours at Northeastern University and graduated. Finally! Because of my unusual experience, they let me create my own degree. I graduated in a cap and gown the same day Jim got his master's degree from Northwestern. My mom was in the hospital at the time, so Jim and I went there in our caps and gowns and took a picture.

All these things happened in my fifties; those were the best times. I did a lot in my fifties.

# Centre East for the Performing Arts
## Skokie, Illinois

*Old Centre East*

Centre East started in 1980 when high school District 219 decided to close one of the Niles Township high schools because of declining enrollment. There were three Niles high schools in Skokie: Niles East, Niles North (the newest), and Niles West. Since Niles East was the oldest one, they decided to close it.

I attended some meetings, and the district appointed a committee to try to figure out what to do with this high school building; all 100,000 square feet, and in quite good shape. They had built it in stages, beginning in 1938, and we occupied the newest section, which included the auditorium theater, art room, dance studio, and music wing, with four individual rehearsal rooms and a large band room.

The school district had set up a committee to investigate how it could be re-used. They finally decided to sell it. A real estate developer

*My collection of Centre East posters*

offered to purchase it, tear it down, and build condominiums. I suggested to a couple of members of the committee that we could take over the building and use it as a performing arts center, but everyone thought that that was a very far out idea. This developer said he had just completed a large condominium development and invited the committee to go out and see it. The village liked the idea because it would increase real estate tax income.

In the meantime, Oakton Community College was located in some abandoned factory buildings on Oakton Street. They built a small campus on Oakton West. I talked to Illinois Senator Howard Carroll, our state legislator, about leasing portions of the building to us. At the time, he was in charge of all state funding. I even told him my idea for the college moving into the high school.

A new committee explored possibilities. Arlene Bezark from the Fine Arts Commission and I had the idea of turning it into a performing arts center. One day, I attended a cocktail party at Skokie's Hilton Hotel. Among the many guests were Illinois State Senator Howard Carroll and Dr. Koehnline, the president of Oakton Community College. During the event, Dr. Koehnline quietly told me that soon I would get a big surprise.

Most organizations in Skokie knew our plans to open a performing arts center. When Dr. Koehnline called to tell me that Oakton was going to buy this 100,000-square-foot building from the school district, he said they would be willing to give us a lease for the 1,310-seat auditorium, rehearsal rooms, two dance studios, and art rooms. This meant that we would have a home for Centre East, could begin booking programs, open a box office, and begin operating as a performing arts center. And that did happen.

I remember how I met Jeff Ortmann. We were trying to save Niles East auditorium, and Mayor Smith knew that. One day, Mayor Smith

*View from the balcony*

called me and said that he wanted me to meet someone in his office because that person also wanted to save Niles East. He went to school there and felt very strongly about it. His name was Jeff Ortmann.

When I met Jeff, he had just come to Chicago and recently graduated from the University of Illinois where he was the business manager for the university symphony. He was very good in business matters, and he had just become executive director for Wisdom Bridge Theater on Howard Street in Chicago, touted as one of the best in the city. He had taken the second floor of a crummy old building and turned it into one of the hottest theaters in Chicago. They did wonderful shows there and got rave reviews. Many of the actors and directors went on to become major stars and directors, and many had their own TV shows and films.

We had just moved from Babb Street and began making plans to begin operations. The dance studio was on the other side of the building. A Russian woman—Inessa Alexander—and her husband approached us with the idea of renting the dance studio and operating it as a ballet school. She soon built it up to a major dance studio. That was in the 1980s, and the Ballet Russe de Monte Carlo was born, and became known as the International School of Ballet. It is, I believe, still operating in Skokie.

John Nix, the head of the Niles Township School District handled all of the maintenance of the district's schools and the rental of space. They were always getting calls from people wanting to rent the auditorium of the different schools and other rooms. He would turn them away unless they were actually residents of the district. Mostly, he didn't want to be bothered with it, so I went into his office, and he gave me the book showing all the rentals. I made many notes and then said, "John, maybe you could turn those requests over to us. We'll take over the rentals and use that income as operating revenue."

He agreed, and we began renting out Centre East at that point. They didn't give it to the Fine Arts Commission; they gave it to us. I think we had a lease of some sort. We paid some modest rent to the school district and took all the calls the school district received whenever someone wanted to rent an auditorium or special rooms in the building. We also could keep the money from all the rentals. We formed an organization, and Jeff Ortmann chaired it.

When John Nix gave us a lease for the Niles East property, it included the 1,310-seat auditorium, four individual music practice rooms, a large band rehearsal room which seated more than a hundred, the dance studio and art rooms. We named it Centre East for the Performing Arts. We applied for and received our 501(c)(3) from the Internal Revenue Service, got a sales tax exemption from the State of Illinois, formed a board, applied for and became an Illinois corporation. We began offering rental rates, started booking programs, hired a technical director, and began publicizing our shows and letting the world know about our rental spaces. Jeff knew how to accomplish most of that and I learned from him. Remember, I had no background in operating a facility like the one we acquired.

I was there an awful lot but with no salary. We didn't have a staff at first; we had volunteers. I remember Barbara Yusen, a volunteer who handled the rentals. But eventually we began paying people a little bit. We had a small crew to handle the tech stage work. Our first crew was the same high school kids that worked the shows at Niles North High School. They knew how to handle the equipment.

I went there one evening because I needed something from the office. When I pulled into the driveway next to the stage door and went in, I found all these kids playing field hockey on the stage with all the equipment around. I threw them off; I was so angry. There was so much stuff that they could have broken. Then I decided we needed to do better and hire a more professional crew. Some of the kids were very good, so I kept them.

One kid was excellent on the soundboard, and many years later, he married and had had his own family. One day, he came over to thank me for getting him started. He was working in Atlanta for Ted Turner and CNN as their head sound engineer. I never forgot that. I thought it was so wonderful. I thought he was a very nice boy and really a genius with sound.

While everyone involved in Centre East were unpaid volunteers, I thought we needed to hire an experienced executive director as soon as possible. After interviewing many candidates, we decided on hiring a recent graduate with an advance degree in performance venues. We hired one who actually moved up here with his family and started working for us. Even though he had the degree, it turned out to be a big mistake. He did things without consulting the board or me. He kept everything a secret. When we finally realized that we had to let him go, I had the awful job of telling him. It was hard, but it had to be done.

Now what do we do? Someone had to take charge. Even though I had never run an operation like Centre East, I knew what I had to do on a daily basis, and, with Jeff's help, I learned how to run the place. I began to build a staff, book performances, set ticket prices, buy advertising in the major newspapers, develop operating budgets, prepare budgets for individual shows, establish relations with many booking agencies, and more. I began attending national and regional booking conferences and selected a balanced series of performances. Then, by looking at display ads in the major newspapers for ideas, I began working with artists to develop our center's logo and creating the display ads for our series and individual shows. I contacted the Illinois secretary of state and, after many letters back and forth, got road signs on the Eden's Expressway (I-94), directing people to our facility.

Most important was learning about applying for grants. I applied to the Illinois Arts Council, the Village of Skokie, and local corporations and businesses, and we were successful in getting donations to cover expenses beyond our ticket admissions. The grant we received from the National Endowment for the Arts for $10,000 was the one that makes me proudest. It made Centre East for the Performing Arts a nationally recognized Performing Arts Center. Ten thousand dollars was a huge donation in the 80s. Jeff was able to get us an ad page in *Stagebill*, the theater magazine, which was available in every theater in Chicago.

As our audiences grew, so did our reputation, and I was even invited to join the Illinois Arts Council Presenter's Panel. We met in the State of Illinois building downtown and reviewed grant requests from theaters all over the state and accepted or rejected the requests. As part of my duties, I had to visit each requesting organization all over the state. My expenses were covered, and I learned a lot about our state. I served on that board for a couple of years and loved it.

We eventually got a paid crew and hired a tech director named Larry. When we had a show to do and got the tech requirements, he would bring in guys on an hourly basis. Some shows needed a big crew, like a dance company, and some didn't, like a stand-up comedian. All they needed was a mike, a sound engineer, and someone to handle the lights and curtain. I began learning about equipment, grant writing, marketing, promotion, paid advertising, personnel, and eventually I was able to buy better equipment to replace the stuff we had been using. Most of that early equipment was in terrible condition. They were leftovers from the high school when they had moved, and the other schools didn't want any of it. They took the good stuff. We had a black main curtain that had holes in it and an old soundboard, which sometimes wouldn't work, but gradually we replaced it.

In addition to Larry, we had Margaret as his assistant. They were dating each other at the time. She was a woman but very masculine. There had been a commercial theater operating down by Golf Mill called the Mill Run Theatre that presented major acts, but eventually they closed. When that happened, I called them. They said, "Sure, come on and look at the equipment," with the idea that we could purchase it for our theater.

I took Larry with me but told him we didn't have much money to buy things. After looking at it, he told me we didn't really need any of their equipment. Meantime, Larry went back later on his own and bought a lot of their stuff and set himself up in business, renting out the equipment.

We did have some good guys then. One became our crew director— he might still be there. He was roommates with Ken Burns, the award-winning documentary filmmaker, who has produced a number of films for TV about baseball, the Civil War, and more. He was good, and he ran a good crew.

Some of the best people I hired were Nida Tautvydas and Carol Fox. Carol worked part-time at Ravinia when I hired her to work in the box office. She began taking on more responsibilities, and one time I took her to New York with me to the booking conference. But she was ambitious in a lot of ways. The woman who ran Hubbard Street Dance Company hired Carol away from me, and I didn't know about it. The Hubbard Street director apologized later.

Almost from the beginning, I started booking shows. I don't remember how I learned how to do it. At my own expense, I went to booking conferences held all over the country. I met many of the talent agencies and learned which artists and companies were available, their prices, tech requirements, and availability, and I picked the artists I liked and that I thought I could sell to an audience.

I'd always been a fan of Fred Waring and the Pennsylvanians. When I was a kid, I used to listen to his choir on the radio. I loved choral music, and he had a great choir. I booked him one time, and I never forgot that he came with the whole choir. We had the old Niles East High School's theater and the dressing rooms were crummy, but they didn't seem to mind as long as they got their money. We sold every seat.

With every contract, there was what they called a "tech rider" that pretty much spelled out their needs—equipment, sometimes hotel rooms, dinner, and so on. In return, I would receive a thick contract with all their needs. Based on what my crew would cost and what the other needed requirements were, I'd have to decide what the ticket price would be based on my estimate of the potential audience. I developed a formula and assumed a 60 percent sale. Originally, I didn't even know what ratio I should use for pricing tickets. If I had expenses of $40,000, for example, and had 1,310 seats in the theater, what percentage did I think would sell? Many people said 60 percent. Some said 70 percent. I think it was more like 55 percent to break even.

I learned about breakevens from Al. I had to decide on the ticket pricing and some other things. Because we were an arts organization, we applied to the Illinois Arts Commission for grants. We had to book some artistic programs to qualify as an arts organization. We couldn't just have pop performances like Fred Waring, comedians, and movie shows, even though they were the ones that sold out and made profits. For example, modern dance was hard to sell. I booked Philip Glass, a modern composer of very unusual music, which normally would be hard to sell but because everyone in the music world knew about him, he sold out. We had people like that with unusual music and dance programs. The people who bought tickets to these programs were usually dancers or musicians themselves and usually didn't have much money. To make the ticket purchase, I tried to keep the ticket prices somewhat lower than usual.

To learn about all the different companies that were very good, I read reviews. I would book these shows, knowing we'd lose through lower ticket prices, but we were able to secure grants to support these programs from the Illinois Arts Council and other places. I was getting quite good at fundraising. The biggest grant that I ever got was from the National Endowment for the Arts for $10,000, a major amount at that time.

The Chicago Community Trust also was very good to us, and I knew the woman in charge very well. Jeff directed me to several of these places because he was doing the same thing for Wisdom Bridge Theater, and he had a lot more knowledge about all that kind of thing. I lost track of Jeff but saw him many years later at a fundraiser that I attended.

Jeff had a brother Tim, a sister Sue, and another brother Bob. Tim became the head of the theater department at Niles North High School. He took some of his group to the theater festival in Scotland. Jeff also went to the Scotland Theater Festival, and one time he went to a theater festival in Israel. When he was in Israel, he left a briefcase in the cab with money, scripts, and all kinds of valuables in it. He thought, Oh, my God, this is gone forever. But some man not only found it, but called him and kept it for him. When Jeff got it back, not a thing was missing. It was really wonderful.

Jeff was a big help. He and his partner later broke up, but they came over one day to the theater. They went into the coatroom in the

*The box office*

lobby, trashed it, and remade it into a real box office. We built a ticket box with a million little cubby holes for tickets. We actually printed tickets. We didn't have a computerized system; that came along later.

Once, we had a Chinese group, and they brought their own woks to cook in their dressing rooms in the basement. When they left, there remained a lot of smelly garbage. I also remember having to find hotel rooms for a very large group. I remember driving them around the Golf Mill area because there were many inexpensive motels there. They kept looking for the cheapest place they could find. Sometimes Centre East paid for the accommodations, but in this instance, they had to pay for their own hotel.

## Centre East Performers 1979 through 1997

| Date | Performance |
|---|---|
| 11/22/80 | Fred Waring & the Pennsylvanians |
| 1/14/81 | Cole Porter Review |
| 3/21/81 | National Dance Company of Yugoslavia |
| 3/22/81 | Maynard Ferguson Band |
| 4/23/81 | Music of Richard Rodgers |
| 5/2/81 | Up With People |
| 7/11/81 | Corky Siegel/Judy Roberts |
| 8/1/81 | Second City |
| 10/17/81 | 1,000 Years of Jazz |
| 10/21/81 | The Christmas Carol – every year '81to '97 |
| 11/15/81 | Parthenon Dancers of Greece |
| 11/28/81 | Buddy Rich and The Buddy Rich Band |
| 1/82 | Meadowlark Lemon & the Bucketeers |
| 1/10/82 | Ballet Trockadero de Monte Carlo |
| 3/1/82 | The Chinese Magic Circus of Taiwan |
| 3/14/82 | The Desert Song (operetta by Sigmund Romberg) |
| 4/18/82 | La Boheme-San Francisco/Opera's Western Theater |
| 4/23/82 | World of Richard Rodgers with Skitch Henderson |
| 9/13/82 | Showcase of Performing Arts for Young People every year '82 to '97 |
| 10/14-15/82 | Cincinnati Ballet |
| 10/23/82 | Steve Landesberg |
| 12/11/82 | City Ballet of Toronto |
| 2/4-5/83 | Guthrie Theater |
| 2/12/83 | The Amazing Kreskin |
| 2/19/83 | Arirang Korean Folk Festival |
| 2/23/83 | H.M.S. Pinafore |

| Date | Performance |
|---|---|
| 3/4-5/83 | Pilobolus Dance Theater |
| 3/14/83 | The Desert Song (operetta by Sigmund Romberg) |
| 3/14/83 | Vaudeville – As it Was |
| 3/19/83 | Big Band Cavalcade |
| 4/22-23/83 | Hubbard Street Dance |
| 4/25/83 | Klezmorim (Eastern European Yiddish revival band) |
| 10/1/83 | Bella Lewitzky Dance Company |
| 10/13-16/83 | 1940's Radio Hour |
| 10/28-29/83 | American Players Theater |
| 10/30-31/83 | The Mikado |
| 11/11/83 | The Brass Band |
| 11/12/83 | Landis & Company |
| 11/19-20/83 | Ballet Trockadero de Monte Carlo |
| 11/26/83 | The Smothers Brothers |
| 12/3-4/83 | Myron Cohen |
| 12/8-9/83 | Nutcracker-City Ballet of Toronto (every year '83 to '97) |
| 2/26/84 | Vienna Choir Boys |
| 3/23-24/84 | Murray Louis Dance |
| 4/26/84 | Myron Floren & Company |
| 5/12/84 | Chicago Repertory Dance Ensemble |
| 5/26/84 | Billy Crystal |
| 6/3/84 | Glenn Miller Band |
| 9/13/84 | CLIO Awards-every year till 1990 |
| 10/13/84 | Dimitri |
| 10/14/84 | Jane Russell in Stars & Songs |
| 10/16/84 | Scandia Festival |
| 10/21/84 | PDQ Bach |
| 11/2/84 | Gabe Kaplan in "Groucho" |
| 11/9/84 | Ray Charles |
| 11/13/84 | Twyla Tharp Dance Company |
| 11/23/84 | The Hit Paraders |
| 12/8/84 | Tommy Dorsey Orchestra |
| 2/9/85 | Chuck Mangione Band |
| 3/1/85 | National Theatre of the Deaf |
| 3/2-4/85 | Shalom '85 – every year till '88 |
| 3/8-9/85 | Pilobolus Dance Theatre |

| Date | Performance |
|---|---|
| 3/16/85 | Ballet Mexican Folklorico |
| 3/19/85 | American Ballet Comedy |
| 3/30/85 | Anna Russell (opera satirist) |
| 4/3/85 | Some Enchanted Evening with Edie Adams |
| 4/10/85 | The Brass Band |
| 4/20/85 | Polish Chamber Orchestra |
| 4/21/85 | Northern Illinois Jazz Band |
| 9/20/85 | Ray Charles |
| 9/28/85 | David Brenner |
| 10/2/85 | The Best of Burlesque |
| 10/12/85 | Gypsy |
| 10/19/85 | Ferrante & Teicher (piano duo) |
| 10/30/85 | They're Playing Our Song |
| 11/2/85 | Ars Musica |
| 11/3/85 | Aman Folk Dance Ensemble |
| 11/9/85 | Ray Charles |
| 11/16/85 | National Theatre of the Deaf |
| 11/17/85 | The American Dance Machine |
| 11/30/85 | Yakov Smirnoff (Russian comedian) |
| 2/13/86 | Betty Buckley |
| 3/1-2/86 | Shalom '86 |
| 3/3/86 | Mantovani Orchestra Salute to Mario Lanza |
| 4/19/86 | Rita Moreno |
| 6/7/86 | Cleo Laine |
| 9/20/86 | Steve Allen |
| 9/28/86 | Cloudgate |
| 10/26/86 | Frankie Laine/Kay Starr |
| 11/1/86 | Alan King |
| 11/23/86 | Cleo Laine |
| 11/28/86 | Richard Lewis/Kenny Rankin |
| 1/16-17/87 | Joyce Trisler Dance Company |
| 2/6/87 | Tony Bennett |
| 3/29/87 | Ballet Eddy Toussaint |
| 4/4/87 | Robert Klein |
| 7/18/87 | Hal Linden |
| 8/1/87 | Chicago's Hottest Comedians |

| Date | Performance |
|---|---|
| 8/1/87 | The Alchemedians |
| 10/29-30/87 | Imago |
| 11/8/87 | Rich Little |
| 11/28/87 | Rosemary Clooney Christmas Show |
| 11/29/87 | La Troupe Circus |
| 12/5/87 | Mummenschanz |
| 12/31/87 | Lainie Kazan – New Year's Eve Special |
| Jan. 1988 | Sports Writers on TV |
| 1/14/88 | Keith Brion and his Peerless Sousa Band |
| 2/11/88 | Steve Landesberg |
| 2/14/88 | Eddie Fisher in Concert |
| 3/6/88 | Big Band Gala |
| 3/18-19/88 | Momix Dance Company |
| 4/9/88 | Shelly Berman |
| 4/17/88 | Philip Glass Ensemble |
| 5/13/88 | Elayne Boosler (also 11/27) |
| 10/1/88 | Pat Paulsen |
| 10/2/88 | Michael Feinstein |
| 10/5/88 | Philip Glass "1,000 Airplanes on the Roof" |
| 10/8/88 | New England Ragtime Band |
| 10/21/88 | Chuck Mangione |
| 10/26/88 | 4 Girls 4 |
| 10/28/88 | Les Ballet Jazz de Montreal |
| 10/29/88 | Mark Russell |
| 10/30/88 | Phantom of the Opera |
| 11/3/88 | Natl. Dance Co. of Senegal |
| 11/11/88 | Canadian Brass Band |
| 11/12/88 | Mort Sahl |
| 11/26/88 | Elayne Boosler |
| 12/17/88 | Joan Rivers |
| 12/31/88 | Lainie Kazan – New Years! |
| 3/3/89 | The Big Band Classics |
| 3/5/89 | The Fabulous Four |
| 3/10/89 | Mantovani Orchestra |
| 3/10/89 | Mark Russell |
| 3/11-12/89 | We Are Here - Israeli review |

| Date | Performance |
|---|---|
| 4/8/89 | Mummenschanz |
| 4/8/89 | Preservation Hall Jazz Band |
| 4/14/89 | Dave Brubeck |
| 5/18/89 | Shecky Greene-2 shows (6:30 & 9:30) |
| 9/8/89 | Buddy Hackett |
| 9/29/89 | Flying Karamazov Brothers |
| 10/28/89 | Suzuki Talent Tour |
| 11/3/89 | American Dance Machine |
| 1/12/90 | Ballet Trockadero de Monte Carlo |
| 2/10/90 | The Gatlin Brothers |
| 2/18/90 | Mel Torme/Helen Reddy |
| 3/4/90 | Klezmer Conservatory Band (Boston Klezmer band) |
| 3/11/90 | The Chieftains |
| 3/17/90 | Mummenschanz |
| 3/30/90 | The Tamburitzans |
| 10/5/90 | The Smothers Brothers |
| 10/20/90 | Christopher Parkening |
| 11/17/90 | Gary Burton Quintet |
| 01/20/91 | A Salute to Irving Berlin |
| 02/17/91 | Crystal Gayle |
| 01/19/92 | Avner the Eccentric |
| 03/26/92 | Kathy Mattea |
| 06/04/92 | Brett Butler |
| 02/20/93 | Irish Rovers |
| 03/17/93 | Jackie Mason |
| 04/17/93 | Carol Leifer |
| 12/03/93 | George Winston |
| 02/17/95 | Bobby McFerrin in Concert |
| 03/31/96 | Joel Gray |
| 11/7/96 | Marvin Hamlisch |
| 11/30/96 | Al Franken |
| 02/28/97 | Boys of the Lough |
| 03/01/97 | Coasters, Drifters & the Platters |
| 03/09/97 | Alice in Wonderland |

## Undated Shows

| | |
|---|---|
| American Indian Dance Theatre | River North Dance Company |
| An Evening with Art Hodes (jazz pianist) | Robert Merrill & Roberta Peters |
| Blackstone, the Magician | Romeo & Juliet |
| Bob Goldthwait | Roseanne Barr & Louie Anderson |
| Bolcom & Morris | Sammy Cahn |
| Chicago Repertory Dance Ensemble | Sankai Juku Dance |
| Count Basie Band | Shenanigans |
| Dracula: The Ballet | Shikisha (South African dance group) |
| Ellen Degeneres | Shirley Jones in Concert |
| From Russia to Israel | Siegel/Schwall Band |
| Harry James Band | South Pacific |
| Hubbard Street Dance | Stars of the Lawrence Welk Show |
| Hungarian State Folk Dance Company | Taming of the Shrew |
| Jerry's Girls | The Capitol Steps |
| Julius LaRosa/June Valli | The Golden Boys-Frankie Avalon, etc. |
| Ken Matthews Show | The King's Singers |
| Kenny G | The Lettermen |
| Kodo Drummers | The Mamas & The Papas |
| Le Dortoir (Dance) | & The Kingston Trio |
| Lee Greenwood | The Pajama Game |
| Legends in Concert | Three Stooges Festival with "Jump in the |
| Louise Mandrell | Saddle" Band |
| Marilyn Michaels | Tom Chapin |
| Midsummer Night's Dream | U.S. Air Force Band |
| Mur Mur Dance | U.S. Army Field Band and Chorus |
| Paula Poundstone | U.S. Navy Band |
| Peter Nero & Robert Merrill | Urban Bushwomen |
| Peter Schickele in Concert | Victor Borge |
| Philip Glass' "Koyaanisqatsi" | |
| Phyllis Diller | |
| Pirin-the Bulgarian State Dance Company | |
| Red Star Red Army Chorus | |
| Richard Jeni | |
| Rita Rudner | |

In addition to the regular shows above, there were these shows aimed at younger audiences:

## Centre East Youtheatre and Family Theatre

| | |
|---|---|
| Aladdin | Not So Dumb |
| Androcles & the Lion | Nutcracker |
| Babar | Peter and the Wolf |
| Babes in Toyland | Pinocchio |
| Ballet Hispanico | Play to Win |
| Bob /Maria of Sesame St | Potato People |
| Buffalo Shufflers | Raggedy Ann & Andy |
| Charlie and the Chocolate Factory | Rumpelstiltskin |
| Charlotte's Web | Sherlock Holmes |
| Cinderella | Snow Queen |
| Emperor's New Clothes | The Amazing Einstein |
| First Lady | The Chinese Circus |
| Footprints on the Moon | The Hobbit |
| Freedom Train' | The Jungle Book |
| Hansel & Gretel | The Secret Garden |
| Hershel and the Hanukkah Goblins | Treasure Island |
| Houdini | Twas the Night Before Xmas |
| Hunting of the Snark | Ugly Duckling |
| International Festival of Children's' Films | Up With People |
| Jack & the Beanstalk | Velveteen Rabbit |
| Kaze Noko | We Have Stories West Africa |
| Lady Liberty | We the People |
| Little Theatre of the Deaf | West African Celebration |
| Martin Luther King | Wind in the Willows |
| Mother Goose Review | Wizard of Oz |
| New Kid | |

Here are my memories of some of these people and their performances at Centre East:

## THE MIKADO

Al and I were tremendous fans of England's D'Oyly Carte (Gilbert & Sullivan). When we booked The Mikado to play at Centre East, knowing we both were Gilbert & Sullivan fans, they dressed us up in Japanese costumes, and we both were in the show. We held up the canopy that the Mikado walked through when he entered.

## STEVE ALLEN

I never forgot that I learned he was very tall. You see, I booked people I liked. But he wasn't very pleasant; maybe he wasn't feeling good or whatever, but he did a good show. He asked to make sure audience members filled out cards in advance with questions, and then I would give him the cards before he started. He was very good at ad-libbing. I went down into the dressing room to talk to him. He was trying to take a nap on a loveseat but because he was over 6' tall and the loveseat in that room was only about 5' long, his legs were hanging over the end. It was really very funny.

## BUDDY RICH

One of the world's greatest drummers brought his band for an evening of contemporary sounds and a reprise of some of the old favorites. A very popular drummer who got a standing ovation, but when it came to that moment when the audience wanted an encore, he would not come out from behind the curtain. Not so nice.

## COUNT BASIE

When he was due to go on, the audience was all in their seats but no Count Basie or the band or anything. I didn't know where he was, so I began calling everywhere. Finally, the stage door opened and some old man who hardly could walk, worked his way across the stage to the piano bench. "We're ready," he said, and the band got into place. They knew what to do right away; they didn't need to rehearse. The show began, and he was wonderful. He perked up once he was on stage. He was a very old, tired man, but he did a terrific show.

**BILLY CRYSTAL** was great. A month or two before his scheduled performance, his agent from the William Morris Agency called me, saying that they had to cancel because Billy Crystal had just been invited to be on *Saturday Night Live*. He was just getting started; he wasn't well known. The only show he'd been on was a TV series called *Soap* for which he played the role of Jodi, a homosexual. In fact, when I booked him, and our ad said that Billy Crystal was coming, people would ask, "Who's he?"

When I learned he had to cancel, I scrambled to come up with a substitute program. I came up with the idea of a Three Stooges Festival. There was a Detroit singing group called Jump in the Saddle. In reality, they were firemen or policemen, known for the song, *The Curley Shuffle*, so I booked them along with Jeffrey Forrester, the author of a popular book about the Three Stooges, and I got in touch with him. He came, talked about the Stooges, and showed film clips from some of their movies. It was a great show and it sold out. You know, we had about two weeks to pull it all together.

And then Billy Crystal came back and performed at a later time. He made a deal with us where he waived his fee of about $6,000 and did his show for nothing. His appearance on *Saturday Night Live* really started his great career. When I picked them up at the airport, I remember that he wanted to go back to LA that night after the show because his two daughters were in a Little League game. He called the airports, but they didn't have any flights to LA after 10:00, so it turned out that he couldn't make the game; he was a little upset about that. (Jim remembers getting up very early Sunday morning and picking Billy up at the purple Hyatt Hotel so that he could get to O'Hare for the first flight out to L.A. A very, very nice person.)

But as I was driving him to the Niles East building, he noticed the audience arriving and commented on all the gray-haired people. He adjusted his show to appeal to that kind of audience. He did the most wonderful show, but his material was great for the younger people also. His line "You look mahvelous, darling" started then. Just a great, great show. I enjoyed it. I sat down in the audience and laughed and laughed. We didn't have any empty seats; he was that good.

Nancy Stevens was my main agent at the William Morris Agency. We had met first at a booking conference in New York and became very close friends. She was a big agent at William Morris and was the one that was dealing with me on Billy Crystal. I got to know many agents and worked with them, booking my major acts. I was quite good with them. I didn't haggle too much. I learned the importance of negotiating fees a little bit, as well as the things the talents asked for in the riders.

**JOAN RIVERS** was on the downhill when I booked her, and she arrived with just a secretary named Dorothy, no one else. The tech rider that I had received from her originally requested that we have a steak dinner for twelve people with a white tablecloth, china dishes, and all that stuff. I said we can't do that, nor do we even have the facilities to do that. I talked to Nancy, and she said to forget it. That's when Joan was doing these big shows and making those demands.

Joan came to me at one point and said, "Do you think I could get a hamburger somewhere?" She put on her mink coat before the show, went outside, and walked around the block a little bit. We were located in a residential neighborhood, and if someone saw her walking there in her mink coat and said, "Hey, that's Joan Rivers," it would have been so funny. She was just a nice person.

In fact, my son Jim was at that show with Doris who was pregnant with Brian. After the show, Doris went into labor the next morning and went to the hospital. I told Joan Rivers that I think she made her laugh so much that it brought on the delivery. It made a good story.

She had lived in LA and then in New York. She had a gorgeous apartment in New York, and her daughter Melissa had a beautiful house in Los Angeles where she lived with a man for years and years. And she had a child, Joan's only grandson. She went for a visit there, and Melissa said, "Why don't you stay for a while?" And she did. Of course, she started running the whole house. This became a great TV series and mostly adlib, I think. I really do. It was mostly what was happening.

We had **PHYLLIS DILLER** too. I remember going backstage to talk to her, and the lights were very low. I tried to see evidence of all the plastic surgery she had had done. She looked good in the dark, but she was old.

When we had **ALAN KING**, an audience member asked if he could meet Alan King backstage and say hi to him. "Oh, he knows me," the person said. "He knows me very well." I told Alan King, and he said, "Oh, that guy. He put me in touch with someone to adopt a baby because we didn't have children, and he screwed it up really bad. I don't want to talk to him ever again." Alan King and his wife actually adopted a baby from the famous place, The Cradle in Evanston. He had a couple of kids from there.

**JACKIE MASON** disappeared after the first show, and nobody knew where he had gone. He was set to do two shows that night. He went to a restaurant and talked to everyone there, but none of us knew where he was. He had even sent the limo driver away. Anyway, we finally got them back to do the second show, but he was such a flighty guy. He was very smart also. He told me he had once studied to become a rabbi.

**MYRON COHEN** was very good, an old, old man in his eighties. He traveled with a woman and told me that she was his nurse. She had to give him a vitamin B-12 shot before every performance. I don't know if she was a nurse or a girlfriend, but he did get the shot.

And then there was **SHECKY GREEN**, a miserable guy and not a very nice person. He was from Chicago, and his brother and sister-in-law lived near the high school. Shecky had to have an orchestra to play as he came on stage. Did he sing? I don't think so. I remember being backstage, and he was haranguing me about something he wanted, and he wasn't very nice about it. I actually answered him back, and the sister-in-law said, "I'll take care of him." And she balled him out, "Come on. Let's stop this nonsense." After that, he was okay to us. I never forgot that part.

**BUDDY HACKETT** was separated from his wife at the time. He had a friend who lived on Marine Drive, and he stayed there. They came to the theater together, so we didn't use the limo. And when they came to the stage door, his friend had a shirt hanging on a wire hanger. Buddy asked if someone could iron it for him. So I took the shirt home, washed it, and ironed it. I brought it back to the theater, and he wore it that night. He also told me, "I don't want to see any children in the audience, and if there are any, put them way in the back because I don't want to see them. I do very blue material." A woman in a front row seat was very pregnant. He had her stand up. He went off the stage and went over to her. And he said, "Oh, that's a pretty dress. May I touch it?" She said, "Oh, yeah, I guess so." And he touched her big belly and got a big laugh out of the audience. He did that kind of material, but he was very funny.

The same thing happened with **JOEL GREY**. Somehow, his underwear needed washing, and he wore boy's sizes because he was a little guy. I remember taking it home to wash it. I got a white box with tissue paper, which I wrapped around his underwear and put it in a box. I even wrapped the box and put a bow on it. When I gave it back to him, he thought that was good.

One of the funniest acts I booked was **MARK RUSSELL** and his one-man show. He was known for his series of PBS specials that aired live at least four times a year between 1975 and 2004. His specials were a mix of political stand-up comedy covering current events and musical parodies. He always sang and accompanied himself on his trademark American flag-themed piano. He used our Steinway and brought his flag with him. He was particularly well known for making fun of Democrats, Republicans, and sometimes a third party, independent politicians, and other prominent political figures. I booked him several times, and he always sold out.

He used melodies from old standards; for example, following the execution of Romanian dictator Nicolae Ceausescu, Russell did a parody to the tune of *Chattanooga Choo-Choo* (Pardon me, boys/ Are you the cats who shot Ceausescu/You made my day/The way you blew him away). He admitted that most jokes and songs were very topical and had "a shelf life shorter than cottage cheese." When asked, "Do you have any writers?" his standard response was "Oh, yes. I have 535 writers, a hundred in the Senate and rest in the House of Representatives!" By the way, he is a classically trained pianist. He retired but continues writing. I wish I could turn back the clock and sit through another one of his wonderful performances.

## DANCE COMPANIES

We had many dance companies—modern-ethnic, classic, jazz, etc. I remember thinking about these professional dancers, and when I saw them backstage, they ate garbage food and stood around smoking. They were very young and very good, but how awful what they were doing to their bodies.

**BALLET TROCADERO DE MONTE CARLO** was a huge all-male ballet company, and they were so funny. I was backstage, and one of them put a basketball inside of his costume so it looked like he was a pregnant ballet dancer. He was wearing a tutu and the complete ballet outfit. They were wonderful ballet dancers. It was the only time they'd been in Chicago, and I was the one who had brought them here. They were a big hit, so I brought them in several times.

The **CAPITOL STEPS** had never appeared in Chicago before I brought them here, and they were a huge hit too. They're still great and a guaranteed sell-out. They wanted to know about the politics of Skokie, so they could throw in a gag about it, but mostly they were doing stuff about Chicago, but they needed that kind of hook.

Of course, *The Nutcracker* always sold out, and I booked many different companies during the Christmas season to perform this classic. No matter which company performed it, it was always a sell-out.

We always had national and Chicago companies performing classical or modern dance along with international touring groups from Greece (Parthenon Dancers), Mexico (Ballet Folklorico) Aman,

Senegal, Canada (Les Ballet Jazz de Montreal), Bulgaria, Hungary, France, and Japan (Sankai Juku).

I also booked Chicago's very popular **HUBBARD STREET DANCE COMPANY,** also a guaranteed sell-out. However, not every dance performance was profitable.

While the productions were fantastic, most dance companies lost money for us. But, as we were known as an arts presenter, we were eligible with our "artsy" programs to apply for and receive grants from the Illinois Arts Council and once from the National Endowment for the Arts, something I was very proud of. These grants helped cover some of the expenses of presenting these companies.

## CLASSICAL PERFORMERS

I had a show with **Robert Merrill and Roberta Peters**, famous opera singers. When I was part of the *Women in the News* newsreel in 1945, Roberta Peters was also on that one. I gave Roberta an extra a copy of *Women in the News*, but she wasn't very gracious about that gift. Robert Merrill was a Cubs fan, and he wanted a TV so he could watch the Cubs game. He was a very nice man. I remember sitting down in the dressing room and just chatting with him about a lot of stuff.

## FRED WARING AND THE PENNSYLVANIA

I'd been a choral singer most of my life, starting in eighth grade. I thought I was quite good and had set my sights on someday singing with Fred Waring and the Pennsylvanians. Waring was considered king of popular choral music. When Centre East began, my first booking was Fred Waring and the Pennsylvanians. I was so excited when their bus pulled up in our stage door driveway. He came with his full orchestra and chorus and gave us a thrilling performance.

## ANNA RUSSELL

Anna Russell was an opera singer, who became famous for her satire and parodies of opera singers. She gave many concerts in which she sang and played comic musical sketches on the piano. Among her best-known works are her concert performances and famous recordings of *The*

*Ring of the Nibelungs (An Analysis)*—a humorous twenty-two-minute synopsis of Richard Wagner's "Der Ring des Nibelungen" and, on the same album, her parody, "How to Write Your Own Gilbert and Sullivan Opera." She became known for her deadpan humor, including her disbelieving emphasis of the absurd in well-accepted stories and her mockery of pretension. For example, in her humorous analysis of Wagner's Ring cycle, she began by noting that the first scene takes place in the River Rhine: "*In* it!!" After pointing out that a character in the Ring cycle was the first woman that Siegfried had ever met who was not his aunt, she pauses and declares, "I'm not making this up, you know!" This phrase also became the title of her autobiography, published in 1985.

At the end of her monologue, she sang the Rhinemaidens' leitmotif and declared, "You're exactly where you started twenty hours ago!" Besides her Ring and Gilbert and Sullivan parodies, Russell was famous for other routines: "Wind Instruments I Have Known" and parodies of Lieder (*Schlumpf*), French art songs (*Je ne veux pas faire l'amour* and *Je n'ai pas la plume de ma tante*), English folk songs (*I Wish I Were a Dicky-Bird* and *Oh How I Love the Spring*), and English music hall songs (*I'm Only A Faded Rose*). She even stretched to blues and jazz (*I Gave You My Heart and You Made Me Miserable*).

## THE CHINESE MAGIC CIRCUS OF TAIWAN

Amazing acrobats, dancers, jugglers, clowns, and comedians went offstage down to the audience and stacked chairs one on top of another while climbing up on them till they reached the ceiling of the auditorium, about two stories high. The audience was afraid they'd fall.

## CHINESE ACROBATS

No one in the company, except their tour manager, spoke English. One of the acrobats became very ill, so I took him to the emergency room at Skokie Valley Hospital. He was diagnosed with chicken pox. Of course, the hospital had to register him and insisted he give his home address. The poor man spoke no English and felt really rotten. Between the tour manager and me, we convinced the hospital to use the address of the hotel they were staying.

**THE BRASS BAND**, known as the "musical Marx Brothers" and were funny, like Victor Borge. In a hilarious concert, they used brass instruments while doing acrobatics.

## RITA MORENO

Beautiful, talented, and very tiny, Rita asked if we could arrange with a health club so she could do her daily workout. The local club was delighted to accommodate her, and she was happy. She was also afraid to fly into Chicago because she was afraid of terrorists, and instead she flew into Milwaukee, Wisconsin! We had to send a limousine to bring her to Chicago. The cost back in 1986 was $140 each way. Her husband, an LA doctor, paid part of that expense.

## CORKY SIEGEL/JUDY ROBERTS

Corky was a very popular Chicago performer of folk music. He and Sandy became good friends. Corky was a folk singer, but when he fell and twisted his ankle, he asked for some ice, and, of course, we had none and not even have an ice bag. What to do? I went to our old refrigerator, chipped off some ice from the freezer, threw it in a baggie, and all was well.

## SUZUKI TALENT TOUR

Shinichi Suzuki, violinist, created the Suzuki Method, a new way to teach children music. He used what he called "the mother tongue" approach. The student learned to play an instrument before learning how to read music. The approach was to learn by repetition, listening, and an early start. This tour brought us a large group of Suzuki students, ranging in ages five and six to fifteen or sixteen. All had been taught using this method.

Two of Centre East's subscribers had children studying the Suzuki Method. They were so excited to meet these students that they hosted a fantastic party at their Winnetka home. Of course, I was invited. It was a wonderful experience for the children and adults, and even though the students knew no English, they had a great time...so did I!

ᏋᏯ—ᏋᏯ

I also booked touring companies from all over the world—Greece, Mexico, Yugoslavia, Israel, Japan, Poland, Bulgaria, Hungary, Russia, Ireland, France, and Senegal. We also did *La Boheme* with the San Francisco Opera Company, and Shakespeare's *Romeo and Juliet*, *Taming of the Shrew*, and *A Midsummer Night's Dream*.

In addition to Shakespeare, we brought in touring companies featuring Gilbert & Sullivan's *The Mikado* and *HMS Pinafore*; the famous Guthrie Theatre from Minneapolis doing *Talley's Folly*; other touring theater groups doing the *1940's Radio Hour*, *The Desert Song*, *Gypsy*, *The Best of Burlesque*, *South Pacific*; Gabe Kaplan in *Groucho*; and The National Theatre of the Deaf; and so many more.

As a presenter, we had to provide the performers or their companies whatever they needed for their performance—example, tuned pianos, organs, or hotel rooms for the company, certain foods, and sometimes transportation.

I remember one particular thing that happened when I booked **The Amazing Kreskin**, the mentalist. I was having dinner with him and his manager in the restaurant at the hotel where they were staying. Kreskin was going to sign for the bill but had to ask his manager, "What's our room number?" My son Marty was there and was flabbergasted. "He's the mentalist and he can't remember his room number?" He never forgot that.

The big moneymakers were always companies like **Capitol Steps, Vienna Boys' Choir** or the *Nutcracker* at Christmas time. It was a well-known fact that booking any of these performers was "money in the bank."

In addition to booking the main acts, various companies or single performers, like comedians, almost all of them needed an "opening" act, another performing group. I developed a large list of local acts that would do about forty-five minutes at the start of the evening, then we would have a short intermission, and then introduce our major performer for forty-five minutes to an hour.

I started the children's **Youth Theater**, a series of professional touring companies that presented their programs performed during weekdays during school hours. These programs were a huge success. Yellow school buses came from all over Chicagoland. I also started a young persons' program series, called **Family Theater**, held on weekends. I invited many the teachers from the different school districts to a meeting to see what their needs were for the coming school year, and I showed them some of the titles of possible shows. One company in New York really did outstanding shows; they never did a bad one. All children's shows did well. At booking conferences, they had special conferences for youth audiences.

I attended booking conferences in Canada, Kansas City, New York, and Milwaukee, where I would book their shows. We would send the teachers a list of the shows that we were considering booking to select titles that tied into the subjects they were teaching. When possible, we would provide study guides. If it was the **Underground Railroad**, for example, they would study that whole era before coming to the show.

School buses came from everywhere. I had to hire people to direct them. The limo driver and his dad Matt would direct traffic, complete with uniforms and white gloves. One time, they wanted to hire extra help to handle the buses and the children, and I said, "Oh, we can't afford that." Finally, I asked him to give me the uniform and the gloves because I wanted to see what was going on in the parking lot. I went out there, and after watching all those buses and loads of children that had to get off the buses and safely enter the theater, I told him he definitely needed more people. It was just a zoo out there!

When we didn't fill every seat, I would invite developmentally disabled and handicapped people to fill them. One time, a woman couldn't take the music, and she went off the wall in the theater. We had to accompany her out.

Many organizations would rent the theater from us, and that was another source of revenue. Many Jewish groups would use it for fundraisers, especially with Jackie Mason or other Jewish comics like Alan King, Myron Cohen, Shecky Greene or Shelley Berman.

I learned how to hire an orchestra, which was required for some artists, and I learned all about the special people who do that. They hired the orchestra, they knew all the musicians, and they knew how to hire the right combination of musicians requested in the tech rider. I became very friendly with a great woman who did that. She was a tall blonde, a very lovely woman.

*School group lining up for a YouthTheater performance*

At one point, I was asked to be on the Illinois Arts Council Presenters Panel. There we reviewed grant requests and decided which presenters (that's what we were called) received grants and the amounts. As part of our investigation, we had to visit the facility and make recommendations to the panel. I served on the panel for two years. We met in the State of Illinois building. I went to places I had never been before—Joliet, Bolingbrook. Aurora, Waukegan—wherever there was a performing arts center.

Besides the Illinois Arts Council, a group of Illinois presenters would meet after the winter booking conferences and review the shows we were interested in booking. Many times, we'd book together so we could negotiate a better fee. We would meet in January because the booking conference in New York was always just before Christmas. They changed that later, but it was a wonderful time to be in New York City. For someone who would never been to New York, except that one time, it was the most exciting time.

What was most thrilling was that we received free tickets to all kinds of performances. I saw Penn and Teller when they were just starting out. I saw Whoopi Goldberg when she was unknown. Both acts performed in little theaters. I was in the front row, right next to the stage. I saw the talent these people had, and they were just getting started.

We saw all kinds of theater with free passes to everything. Al came with me a couple of times. Once, we were on our way to see a show, and he didn't feel good. We had to go back to the hotel. I don't know if we actually saw that show or not. We would eat in the greatest restaurants and see all these free shows. It was wonderful, really great.

Then Governor Thompson developed a program called "Build Illinois." The idea was to save the centers of small Illinois towns that were dying because shopping malls were taking away the business from the downtown areas. He made grants available and thought that establishing performing arts centers in the old movie theaters would help restore the old downtowns.

Each downtown had to have a performing arts center. That's when the Paramount was founded in the old Rialto movie palace in Aurora. It was so neat to visit these old theaters. The one in St. Charles was where I met Wilma Drummer who was running it for the high school district. It was in an old high school with a beautiful auditorium, so we double-booked shows and reduced the fees we had to pay for the artists and various companies.

For Build Illinois, there had to be local participation matching the states' monies, and the Village of Skokie agreed to help by pledging their support. When that happened, the state would put in matching money. That's how we got the money to build the performing arts center. I wanted it to be built on some vacant land abutting the Eden's highway, but the village had something to say about it because they were putting matching money into it. They wanted it next to the Hilton Hotel on Skokie Blvd. The land was next to a large parking garage. I remember going into the garage, going up to the top floor, and standing by the edge to take pictures of this empty land where the building would go.

When they closed down Niles East and had to tear down the theater and some of the older wings of the building, we had to move. I remember on our last day in the building, I began singing that song, "I Did It My Way." To me, it was me. I did it my way. I did everything my way, and I was the last one to walk out of there and close the doors.

We took pictures when they tore that wing down. I was thinking that the ghosts of all the people who'd been here, all the high school people who'd been here, are floating out in the air. And later all the performers I had brought into that building.

We had to move somewhere. What's there now is only parking and grass. Oakton is still there; they have a satellite campus right there in Skokie. They tore down some of the old buildings of the former high school and left the newer pieces there. That high school was built in pieces. It started in the 1930s. Then they added on in the 1950s. That's how old the auditorium was. Later on, Oakton added some more buildings.

Some Hollywood movies were shot there. Soon after we moved into the building, I had a key from John, the superintendent of schools. He used to drive a school bus in the summer for the day camps that Jim attended. John had been a school bus driver, but he was superintendent of District 68 and became superintendent of District 219. That's how it went.

Late one day, I received a call from someone representing a movie company. He wanted to use some of the high school for a movie that required a high school setting. It was the film *Risky Business*, starring Tom Cruise, who was not well known at that point. I said, "Yes, I can show you around." I had a key that opened every door, so we walked into the hallways, the theater, and everywhere. The following Monday when the offices were open, I went to see the superintendent and told him. He was all excited about it and said, "I'll take it from here," and he worked something out with them.

Then the film crew moved in and built their sets in the old gymnasium. The entire interior of the house was built in the gym! There was a scene in *Risky Business* where Tom is in the shower. There was a long dolly shot moving into the shower. I remember seeing that. And then there was the famous scene where he was dancing in his underwear in the living room, wearing sunglasses. I remember when they filmed that too.

I watched a lot of the shooting. They had their own caterers, and we were invited to eat with them. I didn't get to meet Tom Cruise. He was just a young, punk kid nobody knew. Anyway, my favorite thing

*Tom Cruise dances in* Risky Business

was to show people the set. It made a good tour. I could go anywhere with that key.

There's another scene where Tom's in the living room with a girl at night, and the patio doors blow open, and you could see the whole backyard with trees and grass. One day, they brought in actual trees and grass for that scene. They turned the gym into a sound stage and brought in their own generators and air conditioners.

I remember one other thing. Tom accidentally drives a car into a lake and, when he opens the door, the water pours out with fish. I came to know the prop guy quite well, and he asked me, "Where can I buy a whole bunch of fish, live fish?" I helped him find a place somewhere on the North Shore.

I managed to get Marty into *Risky Business*. In one scene, there was supposed to be a high school wrestling team in the background when Tom Cruise talks to his friend. Marty helped me get wrestlers from Niles North, all friends of his. He was in the scene in the locker room when the camera circles Tom Cruise, but you can't see Marty. His friends were in that scene, but the editor cut him out. I think Marty and his friends even received some payment.

Then I got a call about doing another movie with Danny Kaye. It was going to be called *Skokie* and be about when the Nazis were going to come to Skokie to march. The movie included Danny Kaye, Eli Wallach, and Brian Dennehy. Then they took some of the schoolrooms and turned them into offices or the scenes in the mayor's office. They had someone playing Mayor Smith and someone playing the top lawyer.

The prop man for Skokie asked me where he could get several hundred baseball bats. I guess it was for the protesters to fight off the Nazis, but they ended up not using them.

When the real march was happening, I was in a choir, and we were having a concert at the library that very day. Normally, we would drive over to the library and park and go in there. We were wearing our long black skirts and white blouses, and the men were wearing their black pants and white shirts. We couldn't get in. We had to park blocks and blocks away and walk through the crowds that were assembling because the Nazis were going to march. Of course, the village hall was next to the library. There was a grassy village green between them. So there we were in our formal attire, carrying our music and marching right down the middle of that crowd. Everything was rather scary.

Ken Eidson was our conductor. Before the concert began, he said something like, "I'm not even Jewish so they won't bother me." We had a good concert. The audience had to march through everything to get there.

In the film, Joel Grey played a Holocaust survivor who was a resident of Skokie. He wanted to know if anybody could get him a bowl of good chicken soup. And so the girl who worked for me—she wasn't Jewish—said she would make chicken soup for him. I think what he really wanted was chicken soup with matzoh balls, and I would have known where to get some. But she brought him her own chicken soup, and he was gracious enough to enjoy it.

People who worked for me included Barbara Yusen; Nida; Julia, who was originally from Kentucky; and Gail, my secretary, a great woman who helped arrange many things for our fortieth anniversary party, which my kids did as a surprise party on the Centre East stage. They arranged for Al and me to come to the theater on some pretense of a problem, and when we got there, then they pulled the curtain back, and all our friends and family were on the stage and yelled, "Surprise!"

(But of course the surprise was on them as well because, just before they did that, Al said he had left something in the car and went to get it. So when they opened up the curtain, it was just me!) Gail's husband was a fireman in Evanston, and when he retired, they sold their home in Skokie and moved to Sarasota, Florida. I kept in touch with her for a while; she had two daughters. Later on, I heard that they had gotten married and had kids. Gail was a great person.

There was a woman who had French-sounding name, Manette St. Lager. She worked for us in the office, and she was a singer. She had a beautiful soprano voice. She sang at Marty and Karin's wedding. The ushers were mostly older Jewish folks who volunteered in order to see our shows free. They didn't want to usher for the dance and classical music shows. They mostly wanted to see stars and Jewish comedians. We had to design a system that required them to usher for so many less popular shows so they could usher for the "pop" shows. They truly were characters, and Sandy was in charge of them because in addition to doing PR, he was also house manager. He had to give them assignments, but some of them didn't want to walk up the stairs to seat people. They were always arguing amongst themselves.

I had enlarged photos of many of our stars, hanging on the walls in the lobby. When we closed Centre East, the ushers wanted to take those pictures home with them. I said, "Oh, no. I'm taking those." Gail was smart. She always managed to get a picture with one of the artists, and they would sign it to her. I just got the publicity photos but never got around to getting them signed. I was too busy.

Millie Green volunteered at Centre East as an usher; she also ran the concession stand. The ushers were hilarious. Millie would make decaf coffee and regular coffee; the older audiences wanted decaf. One night, she ran out of decaf, so she was going to pour regular coffee into the decaf pot. I said, "Some of these people are going to get sick. You can't do that." She had quite a few little gimmicks that she enjoyed. Then her husband died and she was alone, but that responsibility was like a lifesaver for her. Many people crossed the paths of Centre East.

*Millie, her husband, and an unknown volunteer*

## Sandy Litwin's Centre East Memories

**BACKSTAGE FRENZY**

The first show I ever experienced after beginning my job at Centre East was the opening night of the 1989-90 season, featuring Buddy Hackett. I don't remember the exact date, but it was in September 1989. His son Sandy Hackett was his opening act. I picked Sandy up at the airport. He seemed to be a very arrogant, unpleasant person. Later, in the show, he was just not very funny.

Buddy Hackett was so intense during his performance that he couldn't "unwind" right away after the show. Backstage, many visitors and people wanted to say hello. He was running around from person to person, talking non-stop "Hello! Did you enjoy the show? Nice to meet you!" And so forth. This went on for about twenty to thirty minutes before he asked that we get rid of all the visitors, and he then finally began to calm down.

## MISSING PERSON

When Jackie Mason was scheduled to perform, advance ticket sales were very good; in fact, it may have been a sellout. About three or four hours before the show was scheduled to begin, we received a phone call from his manager or agent that his plane was delayed and he would be unable to make it for the show. Immediately, we sent people to the parking lot to advise arriving attendees of what had happened. I also alerted Barry Solomon at MR. B's TICKET SERVICE because they had sold some of the tickets. In a brilliant move, someone went to BARNUM AND BAGEL to announce the cancelled show to any of our audience that would be there for a pre-show dinner. Some people still showed up for the performance, and most of them were very understanding. Jackie Mason did return to perform a few weeks later and even mentioned the incident during his performance.

## RICHARD JENI'S CONTRACT

When comedian Richard Jeni scheduled a performance, his contract rider had specified nothing that he needed backstage before or after the show. When he arrived backstage, however, he immediately began complaining that there was nothing in his dressing room—no food, no water, nothing. I tried to reason with him. "Just tell me what you need, and we'll get it for you." He continued to gripe and complain. Of course, we found out years later that he suffered from depression and was bipolar, and this contributed to his untimely demise.

## CRYSTAL GAYLE'S HAIR

Country music star Crystal Gayle was known for her great music as well as her long, long hair. Backstage before the show, I learned that one of her sisters always traveled with her because it took both of them forty-five minutes to do her hair before each concert. I also learned that she is very short, barely five feet tall. After her concert, she always did a "meet and greet" backstage with fans, but first she asked me to hold the fans until she could change clothes. It turned out all she really wanted to change was her shoes, which had very high heels to make her taller. In fact, walking downstairs to her dressing room, she said to me, "I can't wait to change out of these shoes!"

## 60 MINUTES

Singer Mel Torme was very nice and polite to everyone, but his show happened to be on a Sunday night. Mel had a habit of watching *60 Minutes*. He was scheduled to perform at 7:30 p.m. He asked if he could find a TV so he could watch *60 Minutes*. The only TV we had anywhere was a very, very small black-and-white set in the technical director's little office. So, at 6:00, there was big star Mel Torme watching *60 Minutes* on a tiny black-and-white TV.

## ALICE IN WONDERLAND

One of our Family Theater shows was a unique presentation of *Alice in Wonderland*. The producer/director had auditions for local kids to play all the parts and then rehearsed for about a week before the show. The day of the show, the music started playing, and nothing happened. The taped music kept playing on and on for about ten minutes, but the curtain never opened. The audience kept getting more and more restless. Finally, the curtain opened and the show started, and it was absolutely awful. None of the kids in the show seemed to know their lines or have any idea what they were supposed to do. At one point, Alice (or one of the other characters) says, "Where are we?" A co-worker of mine, standing next to me in the theater, responded by whispering "We're in hell!" As house manager, I fielded complaints from a swarm of customers in the lobby. I handed out what seemed like hundreds of complaint forms. These came in handy later, because my mother refused to pay the producer for the show, and he filed a lawsuit to get the money.

## HOLIDAY PARTY

All the ushers for Centre East performances were volunteers, and many of them worked at almost every show. To extend our appreciation for their efforts, we threw a holiday party for them every year. One year, my co-workers and I rounded up a number of small prizes to give out, and we had a few games and contests for the ushers as part of the party. When it came time to give out the trinkets, we could not believe the juvenile and petty behavior on the part of these (mostly) senior citizen volunteers. They argued and fought like kindergarteners over these cheap prizes.

## AVNER THE ECCENTRIC

Avner was a performer who never spoke; his performance was entirely sight gags. He had me help him with one "bit" during his show. Twenty minutes after the show started, I was supposed to "usher" a couple of late-arriving audience members to their seats. Onstage, Avner would observe all of this with a disgusted look on his face and then "re-create" the entire show up to that point in "high-speed" motion. Hilarious. My son Kendall and my stepson Danny happened to be there that night (both about ten years old at the time), so I chose them for this "audience participation" bit. Everything went fine at first. I showed them to their seats while Avner stopped the show, watching everything, and then as I left the theater, instead of taking their seats, Kendall and Danny followed me out!

## SECURITY! SECURITY!

The Smothers Brothers show had a first act, then an intermission, followed by a second act where the brothers mostly reverted to their origins as folk musicians. At the end of the first act, as they were leaving the stage, a woman from the audience walked on to the stage and tried to follow them backstage. Some of the ushers were able to grab her before she could go anywhere. I really don't know what she had in mind. Later, backstage, Tom Smothers complained about the lack of security, demanding that we do a better job of protecting him from any "nuts" that might be in the theater.

## I LOVE YOUR TIE

Brett Butler was a standup comedienne whose own TV sitcom, *Grace Under Pressure*, ran for a few years. When she appeared at Centre East, accompanying her was a very annoying tour manager whose main function seemed to be to growl and snarl at anyone who came near her or Brett. As house manager that night, I happened to be wearing one of my many Three Stooges ties. When I went backstage, the annoying tour manager seemed scarcely able to tolerate my presence, but Brett Butler, observing my tie, laughed hysterically, saying, "That's a great tie! I'd like to have one like that myself."

## TOPICAL HUMOR

The political satire group, **The Capitol Steps**, appeared annually at Centre East for many years. One such performance was in March 1994 (or maybe 1995), and I was to drive some of them from the hotel to the theater. One of the guys always did a bit based on switching the first letters of words for comic effect. For example, instead of "British tabloids" he would say "Tittish brabloids." He would then launch into a long monologue, using this technique, discussing not only political issues but anything that happened to be in the news at the time. This particular day was when Michael Jordan announced the end of his baseball career and return to the Bulls. On the ride from the hotel to the theater, the Capitol Steps and I discussed this and turned it into a routine that they used in that night's performance. Some of my contributions included "Atrick Pewing," "Barles Charkley," and the one I'm most proud of, "Pottie Skippen and his fechnical towels!" I always felt I should have gotten writing credit for that.

## BOBCAT'S CHILDHOOD

When comedian Bob "Bobcat" Goldthwait appeared, a number of people wanted to go backstage after the show to say hello or get autographs. He was very accommodating, and most of the people left after just a minute or two. One man, about the same age as Bobcat, was originally from Syracuse, New York (Bobcat's hometown), and they had grown up and gone to school together. This guy had a number of class pictures from the school they had attended, and both he and Bobcat were in each picture. Bobcat remembered the guy whom he hadn't seen in more than twenty years.

## SANDY'S RENTAL MEMORIES

I was house manager for many of the "rental" shows at Centre East during my time there from 1989-1997. I don't have a lot of memories about specific incidents during those events, but a couple come to mind:

## THE "DIAMONDS?"

This was a "pyramid scheme" type sales organization that sold…what? I can't even remember what their product was, possibly some kind of "Herbalife"-type vitamin supplements. They frequently rented Centre East for their meetings that always completely sold out and consisted of award presentations to the top sellers (referred to as "Diamonds"). But most of these meetings were spent trying to whip everyone into frenzy with motivational speeches about the benefits of hard work and increased sales. They even tried once or twice to recruit me as one of their sales men. On more than one occasion, the organizer approached me at the end of the night, thanked me for all my help, and before I could blink an eye, reached out and stuffed $20 into my shirt pocket. I guess these rentals made good money for Centre East, but the people always left me feeling a little dirty.

## ETHNIC FOLLIES

Centre East was always a popular place for shows featuring entertainers from different ethnic cultures, such as Filipino, Russian, Chinese, Polish, and most often Indian/Pakistani. One hot summer night during an Indian show, an altercation broke out backstage, and one person suffered a physical attack and stabbing. Somebody pulled the fire alarm, and we had to evacuate the building. After the Skokie Police restored some semblance of order, the promoters insisted on continuing the show. What no one knew was that pulling the fire alarm automatically shut down the antiquated air-conditioning system, and I had no knowledge of how to restart it. The show went on with more than a thousand people in the audience on a hot night with no air conditioning. Needless to say, it quickly became very hot and uncomfortable.

# Marty Litwin's Centre East Memories

## GLOBETROTTERS

Meadowlark Lemon and His Bucketeers came to the Niles East gym in January 1982. (Lemon, famous leader of the Harlem Globetrotters, had left to form his own group, the Bucketeers.) The show was scheduled for a Saturday night. Well, a blizzard came that day and into the night. The team made it to the gym on time for the game. Not many fans made it through the snow, however. Lemon and his team played the game in front of only about thirty people!

## EYELASHES

In 1982 an impersonator of Liza Minelli rented Centre East for several months for his show. His mother dressed him. During one of his performances, his eyelashes fell off. He stormed off the stage and fired his dresser—his own mother. He refused to go back and complete the show. We had to announce to the audience that the star had had a heart attack, and we were canceling the show. Not everyone wanted their money back, but some did. Thank goodness, it wasn't our show; it was the responsibility of the renter. I don't remember if that incident cancelled the remainder of their leasing contract.

# North Shore Center

The money to build the North Shore Center for the Performing Arts in Skokie came from the Build Illinois program. I felt that Skokie qualified with Centre East, and so I applied. In fact, I went to Springfield when they were going to vote on that bill. The people who were trying to get the bill passed were from other performing arts centers around the state. We had a meeting with some legislators who were arguing about how they could raise some money. They said that they could have a racehorse tax increase. I thought, 'Oh, so that's how things get done.' It was an eye-opener for me. Some people make fun of politicians, but some of them really work hard and try. I was impressed with them.

While we were in Springfield, we attended the House and the Senate and presented our case. It was very interesting.

Back at Centre East a couple of weeks later, we were waiting to hear about the bill. It was a hot summer day, and I received a phone call at about 4:00 or 5:00 p.m. when I was just about to close up. It was Howard Carroll, the senator, and he said, "The state approved a grant for you to build a new theater." He had gotten us $14 million, and then the village came up with some of the money. That's how we began building the North Shore Center for the Performing Arts in Skokie.

The mayor then was Jackie Gorrell. Mayor Smith had died. (If he'd been alive during all of this, he never would have let occur the bad things that happened later. He would have supported the theater the same way that others didn't.) Anyway, we had the money. I was so tired and hot, and I thought, Oh, that's good. I really didn't realize the importance of what he was telling me at the time.

After we received the check, we started looking for an architect.

Many applied, and we flew to Minneapolis, Boston, and other cities to visit architectural firms and see the theaters they had designed and built.

Then I met the people who had done the sound at these theaters. They specialized in only the sound—either the equipment or the structure of the building—the acoustics. I became very good friends with those acoustics people. In one of our meetings, the village said that eight hundred seats were more than enough. We had had one thousand three hundred before, and we were able to book things based on that number of seats. If we didn't have those seats, we would have had to raise the prices or just not book certain shows because 800 seats would limit us a lot. I wanted to have close to 2,000 seats or 1,500 at a minimum. With that many, we could still get some good shows.

An assistant village manager said he didn't want to spend that kind of money because the village would have to pay something more to the total. The sound man said, "No, Dorothy's right. You need to have more seats." I never forgot that he said I was right in front of all those people.

The village man said, "We're not paying you to give us those kinds of opinions." And I said, "What else are you paying him for? He's the expert on sound and theaters." So, we ended up with 815 seats, which was awful.

Then the village made a deal with the hotel so that part of the money went to build an underground passageway between the hotel kitchen and our downstairs so they could carry things up on an elevator. We had this big lobby, but we could have used more seats later on. Eventually, they all said we should have built it bigger; we needed more seats. Oh, well, what can you do? I guess I could have told them, 'I told you so.'

Jackie Gorrell wanted the name to be the North Shore Center for the Performing Arts in Skokie. She insisted we add "in Skokie" to the name. When they closed down the Niles East building, we went into temporary office space in the Green building just behind Old Orchard. There were a lot of medical people in that building, but one of our good ticket buyers owned that building and gave us free office space. Sandy worked there until we were able to move into the new theater.

The village wanted to hire somebody to supervise the building of the theater. I knew the woman who ran the theater down in Peoria, and I asked her for some ideas. She said that a fellow there had wanted to make a change, so he might be interested. He came up and interviewed, and I took him around. The village hired him to supervise the construction. Although I don't know why we needed him. I could've done it. Well, he had experience with that kind of work, and he was a good, smooth talker. I found that out later because I hated him after a while because of the things he pulled.

I pulled up some articles from Peoria newspapers and found out that he had done some very nasty things there. Many newspaper stories about him reported that he had cheated people and so on. Therefore, my feeling about him was legitimate. I took the information to the village, but they were already into it with him.

We finally managed to get the theater built with only eight hundred seats, and we opened. By that time, as with many organizations that start something new, I was the only one doing a lot of the work. But as it succeeds, more and more people say they were there from the

*Front of the North Shore Center*

beginning, they made it happen. That'll happen with the radio station, too, I'm sure. Different people said, "Oh, yeah, I was part of this whole thing. I did this and I did that." It wasn't true. Newspaper stories came out, with the facts always mixed up. It's amazing when a reporter gets things right.

Once we moved into the new building, I didn't have the emotional tie to it. I had a beautiful office on the second floor, and I had a number of people working for me. I brought in Northlight Theatre, and they were just delighted. They were performing in a grammar school in Evanston, so we worked a deal with Northlight and built a small theater and the big theater. We could convert the small theater into an Exhibit Hall for other possible rental uses. My original idea was to have a single convertible theater. In Arizona, we saw a theater designed by an architect that I really wanted to hire. This theater could expand from an 800-seat theater to another 600 with a rotating balcony as they have at Stevenson High School. That's exactly what I wanted because it offered the opportunity to do small things like a lecture or an intimate show or put it all together for a big show. The village voted me down on that.

For a variety of reasons, I ran it for a while and booked the shows, but I never felt connected as I had had with the old Niles East building because we went from nothing into something. An old, old high school building that became well known. Agents all over the country knew that performing arts center.

A volunteer wanted to work for me full-time. I asked her if she could type. She said no. I asked her if she knew how to use the computer. She said no. I needed people who could do things. She was a good talker, and she put together very good parties, but I didn't need that ability, so I didn't hire her. Later, after I left, she "noodged" some people at the village and on our board into hiring her for the executive director position. Then they closed the whole place down and she was out. I called and asked what they were doing. She said, "I don't know what they're doing. They're closing things down." They were foolish because the center had brought a great deal of good to Skokie, good publicity that it wasn't known only as the place where the Nazis marched. Or that Skokie was all Jewish. Or any of those negative things.

# Q&A

Dorothy Litwin is executive director of Centre East for the Arts in Skokie. She helped found the center in 1978 through her work on the Skokie Fine Arts Commission.

*Articles about Centre East*

## Centre East creators leaving posts behind

Two impresarios who turned the Centre East performing arts organization in Skokie into one of the busiest presenters in the area are on their way out— only months after their dream to build the controversial North Shore Center for the Performing Arts came to life last November.

"I'm typing up my letter of resignation right now," said Dorothy Litwin, who created Centre East in 1980. Litwin said she officially would leave her post in the spring. Her son and associate at Centre East, Sandy Litwin, has gone.

Dorothy Litwin last October criticized the village for its scaled-down version of the North Shore Center, a planned 1,500-seat theater reduced to 839 seats on a cramped lot at 9501 Skokie Blvd.

Before the facility was built, the village stripped the Litwins and Centre East of management responsibilities, giving them instead to a Rhode Island organization.

"Without Dorothy, this project wouldn't have been possible," said Mark Vanderpool, assistant village manager.

Why did I quit? I didn't like the way things were going, and Al decided to retire. I decided I would retire too. I think I know what happened. I said something in a publication. One day, a major writer for the *Chicago Tribune* interviewed me. I think I said that I didn't know why they needed to hire an outside firm; we could've handled it ourselves, or something to that effect. That raised such a stink with everybody. I recall going to a board meeting where they just hammered me. I said I don't need this. I'd done enough. They kind of turned against me. I was very disappointed in those people.

They had a big, big party and an outdoor public event where they honored me and gave me gifts. I have a beautiful watch and all kinds of honors. They also put a plaque in the lobby.

*Giving my retirement speech*

*My plaque in the North Shore lobby*

# Waitre D' Deliveries

My retiring from North Shore Center all happened before we moved to Huntley. We bought the Sun City house in 2003 and then moved there in May 2004. So what did I do for the ten years? WAITRE D'! WAITRE D'!

While Marty was pursuing his acting and modeling career, he worked as a driver for ROOM SERVICE, a company that delivered food orders from restaurants to homes and offices in the central part of Chicago. When he had visited Doug in San Francisco, Doug pointed out that there were several such services there in a city much smaller than Chicago. Since ROOM SERVICE was the only meal delivery service in Chicago, Marty decided that he could start another service here and

*Me working at Waitre D'*

came to us with the idea. We gave him some money to get the business going, and we were off to the races. I even came up with the name of WAITRE D' DELIVERIES, a play on the term maître d'.

Marty rented office space near downtown Chicago, and we went there every day. We started listening to books on tape on the long drives, which became a regular thing for us. In that room, Marty would say to the phone, "Ring, please" because he had started with the office and computers, but we had no business at all.

Jim helped a lot with setting up the computers and delivery software. Shortly after we mailed the first menus out, Jim was alone in the office under a desk running wires for the network he had installed. Marty was out in Carol Stream with Karin doing a tasting for their wedding that would happen a month later but had his cell phone in case we received an order. Suddenly, the order phone rang. Jim was so startled that he banged his head on the desk! But he was able to write the very first order down and call Marty with it. Marty recalls that he rushed back to Chicago, changed into his WAITRE D' uniform in the car, and delivered the order. When he mentioned to the customer that it was the first delivery ever for the new company, he couldn't have cared less. He just wanted his food!

That's what made it like Centre East. We started out with nothing and grew. Somebody asked me once why I like to do that. I said I like to be part of something that's developing and growing.

Do you know what Al told me about WAITRE D'? We were in business five years before we sold it. He told me then that we were just beginning to break even. And that surprised me because I thought we were doing so well. We did get back the money we had invested. We had sixty restaurants that used our delivery service. I thought we were really raking in the money.

I remember getting so aggravated when I worked there. Some of the girls that took the orders were horrible. They had no work ethics. They would be eating fried chicken with their fingers while they were on the computer. They would go to our pop supplies in the back and help themselves to free drinks. Just little things. They would be on the phone talking to their boyfriends. I couldn't help it, but I was blowing my top.

If Marty had started the business in this economy, he would have had better quality people. I remember this kid Avery, though, a little guy, was very good. He was a good worker.

There was Jim "The People's Choice" Peoples. He was a good talker, but he'd actually been in jail. He was one of our drivers. And there was Chris who had a high-pitched voice. He started his own delivery business. Quite a few people got their experience with Marty and then started their own business, but I think just a few of them succeeded. Larry and Ralla are still doing it, which was very aggravating to me because they have a home in Highland Park. That should've been Marty.

EZ2Get.com was a Texas company that started buying up restaurant delivery businesses all over the country. Their idea was to centralize order taking and dispatching in Texas and eventually get into delivering other things besides food, like office supplies (an idea which is just now starting to take off). This was during the height of the "dot-com" boom, and Internet companies all had tons of money to spend and didn't care about profits. It was kind of like the Oklahoma land grab. They were all going after traffic to their websites and services at whatever the cost. They came to Chicago and offered to buy both WAITRE D' and ROOM SERVICE, either cash or stock. Most everyone took stock because Internet stocks were riding sky high, but Dad insisted on cash. That was a brilliant move since the dot-com stock crash happened in 2000, and their stock became worthless.

We sold WAITRE D' and then EZ2Get combined WAITRE D' and ROOM SERVICE and made Marty the manager of the combined operations. Marty had built a great reputation with all the restaurants because we paid them all on time (and faster than ROOM SERVICE ever did). Al insisted on always paying them promptly to build our credibility when we started out.

When the dot-com bubble burst, EZ2Get was short on cash. They spent a lot of money building an elaborate call center, but they never really got it right. They didn't have a good feel for the local conditions in each their cities. For example, if there was a snowstorm, the local order takers at WAITRE D' would know to add some time to the estimated delivery time. However, in Texas, they didn't take into account local weather and traffic, so customer service suffered.

What really hurt them was they started not paying the restaurants on time as they ran low on cash. They asked Marty to tell them which restaurants needed money now and which could wait. Marty was in a bad situation there. Larry and Ralla had left to start their own service, and Marty wanted to do the same. However, he was stuck with a contract, so he felt he couldn't leave legally, but I wonder if anybody really would've sued him if he had.

In the end, EZ2Get went bankrupt, and they left owing money to some restaurants. Although most restaurant owners knew it wasn't Marty's fault, he unfairly took the blame for some of it. I know Marty felt bad that the EZ2Get people had ruined the reputation that he had worked so hard to build. If he had left earlier, he could have started over, but we all got money out of the sale. Sandy got a nice piece of change and bought a car and a condominium too.

# Sun City

Marty and Karin had two small children, and their Morton Grove house was getting too small, so they began looking for a larger place that they could afford. The search took them farther and farther west until they found a place in Algonquin, near Elgin and east of Rockford about 35 miles west of Morton Grove.

Al and I had not been thinking of moving, but when Marty and family moved, Al and I started thinking about it. I don't remember what exactly caught my eye, but it must have been some ads for Sun City, a national company that builds homes and operates retirement villages all over the United States.

They made an offer to rent one of their homes for three nights and four days for a remarkable low price of $45 a night with the use of all the facilities while there. We could rent at any of their places, so I suggested we try the one in Las Vegas because my sister, brother-in-law, and niece Sue were moving there. We made a reservation, got confirmation, and flew to Las Vegas. We loved the house and facilities and thought about moving. We went to Sacramento, California, and stayed at another Del Webb facility. It was near San Francisco, so we visited Doug when we completed our stay at that Sun City.

When we returned to Illinois, we decided to sell our home and buy a home in the Huntley, Illinois, Del Webb Sun City. It was a new facility near Elgin and was perfect—near our kids and friends. We finally settled on the Grant model.

Because Sun City had built the house as a "spec" house, it was completely finished—floors, fixtures, tile, colors, built-ins, etc. We liked it very much. Everything was the way we would have selected without having to go through the agony of selecting cabinets, faucets,

*The Litwin boys in front of our Sun City house*

colors, etc.

The 2,300-square-foot house was almost the equivalent of our Skokie house, but this one was a ranch with everything on one floor. It had a basement, three bedrooms, two full baths, an enormous kitchen, a patio, large yard, and an oversized two-car garage.

We had no problem selling our Skokie house. We had signed the purchase papers in Sun City just before Christmas in 2003 and sold our Skokie house in 2004. The real estate market was at an all-time high, so we cleared a little above $100,000 after we bought in Huntley. We sold a lot of our stuff or donated it to various organizations and moved the rest to Huntley.

It was so much fun! It was like starting over—new shopping, new doctors, and new neighbors. Of course, it was the same climate, though. We used the spare bedroom as an office, another as a guest room, and the third and largest as the master bedroom. It was like when we first got married. Al had not been so sure about the move in general, but soon he grew to love it.

Sun City has around a hundred clubs, two outdoor swimming pools, and one indoor pool. It features a beautiful 18-hole golf course, tennis courts, walking and bicycle trails, a fishing lake, and more. Al joined the cribbage club, and we both connected with the Shalom group. There are about a hundred Jewish families, and they held Friday night services in one of the lodges once a month. We got our library cards, opened bank accounts, got our new voter registrations, and had a great time. I signed up with several clubs—computer club, book club, the band, the choir, and a Spanish group.

Oh, I did get involved before the radio station. I was working with Leslie Cowles, helping her with the programming for Sun City. I would introduce these programs and take care of the guest speakers. For example, we had an author who wrote mystery books, I handled everything. She had brought her books there and planned to sell them. I had to handle the money. I also helped Jim start MY LIFE STORY with Al.

"Bumpety, bumpety, bumpety" is all I remember. I was about to go down to the basement to get some memorabilia for my husband's ninetieth birthday party coming up in two days. I was wearing my favorite bedroom slippers. I held on to the railing and stepped down. That's all I remember until I found myself curled up at the foot of the stairs. Doug, who had come in for the birthday party, heard me scream and came running. My husband didn't have his hearing aids in, so he had no idea what had happened. Doug wouldn't let me move. He ran to the kitchen and brought me a half-opened bag of frozen peas that he put on my head and eyes. The twist tie fell off, spilling peas all over me. We laughed and he helped me up to the upstairs couch to rest. I thought I'd call the doctor's office in case he'd like to check me out. The nurse checked with the doctor and said to come in right away. All I could think about was Natasha Richardson who died after a minor fall while skiing.

I could go on about the jokes people made when they saw me. "That's why they call them slippers" or "Let's change the name of the restaurant to Blackeye Grill." That's where the party was to be held. Of

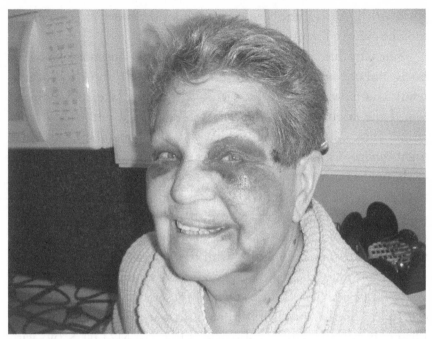

*It looked worse than I felt!*

course, they teased my husband. I could talk about warnings people gave me and other comments. And, of course, I could show some of the pictures people kept taking.

# 101.5 FM – WHRU FM
# Huntley Community Radio

It all started when Allen Pollack from the Shalom group approached me and said, "I know you worked in television a while back, and I've come across something I think you could help me do." It turned out that he and his wife had been vacationing in Florida at a senior retirement place, which had its own radio station, TV station, post office, and a lot more. The fellow at the radio station told Allen about a new program that the Federal Communications Commission (FCC) was offering to small towns that made it possible for them to get a broadcasting license for their own Low Power FM station. Low Power means a broadcast radius of about three to seven miles and a maximum power of 100 watts. They could not sell advertising but could ask for sponsorships, apply for grants, and solicit community donations.

Allen thought it would be good for Sun City and wondered how to proceed. There already was a Low Power station in nearby Round Lake Beach, so we met with those people, examined their operation, and invited them to a meeting at Sun City to explain how we felt that Sun City should get their own radio station. We met with several Sun City people, and Round Lake Beach folks attended the meeting and explained their whole operation. The head of that station was Bish Kryko, and he and his people were a tremendous help. The Sun City group recommended to the Sun City Board of Trustees not to get involved because they felt it would have an impact on their budget and cause an increase in the residents' assessments.

We learned that this program had started back in 2000 and that there were currently around seven hundred LP stations around the country, but under pressure from the existing AM and FM stations, the program shut down. A few years later, a congressional bill opened up the program again, and the FCC rewrote the rules and regulations. In 2009 Congress passed the bill. It went to newly elected President Barack Obama, who signed it, and in 2012 it went to the FCC to rework the rules and regulations. Applications for a license would not become available until they had finished.

When Sun City turned us down, we felt we were done. I suggested we go ahead and let everyone in town know about the opportunity of having a radio station. I suggested we contact all local organizations and present our idea for the station to them too. Allen put together a PowerPoint program, and we began presenting it to the village, park district, library, Rotary and Kiwanis boards, and other organizations.

The idea found wide acceptance. We incorporated as an Illinois not-for-profit organization called Huntley Community Radio LTD and formed a four-person board—Sun City retirees Allen Pollack, Jim Carollo, Pat Molohon, and me. Jim had recently retired after forty-three years as chief engineer at WGN Radio, and Pat was a semi-retired attorney who was also involved in Sun City's theater group. On May 31, 2011, we received our 501(c)(3) status from the Internal Revenue Service, which meant all donations and grants to us were tax-exempt.

One day, we received an invitation to meet with the executive director of the Huntley Park District, Thom Palmer. When we arrived, two of his key people joined us. He said he wanted to show us something and asked that we get into our cars and follow him. He drove to a little brown building within Deicke Park, opened the door, and asked if this area would be suitable for our radio station. WOW! We couldn't believe it. It was a wonderful space with built-in furniture (we just had to get chairs). He was going to rent it to us for $130 a month. We were ecstatic!!!

We decided that we would start out by broadcasting as an Internet station 24/7. I became the program developer. We needed to raise only $25,000 in order to get the basic equipment needed to broadcast on the Internet. My dear Al had recently passed away, leaving me quite a large estate of cash and investments. In his memory, I donated the $25,000, and Jim ordered the equipment, installed it, and in 2012, we went on the air (online).

I lined up programs, and a couple of people who knew what we were doing volunteered to begin programs of their own. Pam Fender, a village trustee, was the first. She called her program *My Huntley Neighbors* and began interviewing folks from the area. Later, she had to give that program up because of personal commitments, so I took it over.

I renamed it *Getting to Know You*, opened with the song with the same title from *My Fair Lady*, and asked a young mother, Anitra Willis, who wanted to get involved with the station, to share the show every other week. We began in 2013, and we have been doing it for the past two years. Together we had interviewed over sixty people when Anitra had to quit in 2014 when she got busy with teaching. I've been continuing until November 30, 2015 when I had a small stroke. Had I ever hosted an interview show? No, but that didn't stop me. I just thought about some of the interesting people I knew or had met and asked if I could interview them on my show. After I got folks to agree to the interview, I first went online to learn all I could about the person or the organization they represented. I prepared an outline of questions, and we were off! I had no problem talking on the radio—it was fun! I have kept it up for almost a year and a half.

Money has always been an ongoing problem for the station. Our yearly operating expenses are considerably modest—under $20,000 a year. It covers our rent, electricity, special services needed to get us on the air, some office supplies, and marketing expenses. Because we are all volunteers, we have no payroll.

We were fortunate that the local medical giant in the area, Centegra Health Systems, wanted to build a new hospital in Huntley and, of course, there was some objection from the existing hospitals. My guess that in order to "make nice" to Huntley, they granted us $10,000—our first outside grant—and they gave us the opportunity to record their monthly physician lectures on various medical subjects. It was our first remote as the lectures were held in a Centegra building and we had to go to the site with all of our equipment. Centegra's grant kept us going our first year.

*Me at the station*

## HUNTLEY RADIO SHOWS AND HOSTS
*(I developed most of them)*

MORNING SHOW.................................. Mike Caserno
THE DINING DUO ................................ Jim & Nancy Eggers
ONCE UPON A TIME ........................... Bill and Carol Waxenberg
HOW DOES YOUR GARDEN GROW?... Kathy Carr
AG NEWS & VIEWS............................... Arlen Higgs
THE DEAN ROWE SHOW...................... Dean Rowe
WHAT'S ALL THE BARK ABOUT? ........ Robin Massey
ENTERTAINMENT SPOTLIGHT .......... Dave Apmann
TENNIS LOVE......................................... Herb Kelly
RAIDER RADIO ..................................... Ann Knipp
KIDS' VIEW ............................................ Ann Knipp

CK SPORTS............................................... Ben Litwin, Cory Knipp,
                                                        Andrew Fulcer
                                                        & Nick Roche
CLASSICAL MUSIC AT ITS BEST .......... Jim Kendros
TWO DUDES AND THE DUCHESS ..... Bill Geheren,
                                                        Kate Curtin
THE HOME SHOW ............................... Mimi Geiger
CENTEGRA PHYSICIAN LECTURES.... Kari Gippert
GETTING TO KNOW YOU .................... Dorothy Litwin
HCR SPORTS ROUND UP ..................... Gary Krewer, Sam Geati,
                                                        Curtis Koch,
                                                        Chris Cunningham
JIMMY'S JUKEBOX................................. Jim Carney
BIG SWINGTIME................................... Joe Alengo
THE BEATLES: Yesterday & Today .......... Rudy K
CRUISIN' MUSIC RADIO ...................... Rudy K
TRUE BLUES ........................................... Tim Erickson
GREG'S CLASSIC JAM............................ Allen Pollack & MCC
                                                        Interns
LOUD AND PROUD ............................. Allen Pollack & MCC
                                                        Interns
THE DORM ROOM .............................. Allen Pollack & MCC
                                                        Interns
CHAINSAW POLKA MADHOUSE......... Jim Kucharski
MUSIC & THE MESSAGE....................... Pastor Bruce Mirash
                                                        St. Peter Church
FINANCIAL STRAIGHT TALK.............. Dave Rosenfeldt
ACCESS WITH RESPECT ...................... Dave Rosenfeldt
WIDE OPEN SPACES............................... McHenry County
                                                        Conservation District,
                                                        Elizabeth Kessler,
                                                        Executive Director
PONDERING OUR PAWS...................... Dr. Debra Junkins, Vet
GARY'S MUSIC HOUR............................ Gary Krewer
RICK'S OLD TIME RADIO .................... Rick Hagerty
ELGIN SYMPHONY ORCHESTRA........ Wendy Evans

THE LISTENERS CLUB........................... Jim Kendros
TABLE TALK.............................................. Paulette Rusk
HOMEMAKING WITH LYDIA............... Lydia Wade
TRAVELIN' MAN ................................... Sam Geati
YOU BOOK IT......................................... Herb Kelly
A LITTLE BIT OF THIS AND A
LITTLE BIT OF THAT........................... Dan Dillman
MCHENRY DEPT OF HEALTH ............ (in development)
VISIT MCHENRY COUNTY................... Jaki Berggren

# My "Getting To Know You" Interviews

*Joseph Loughlin*, retired manager WGN-TV & Hall of Fame broadcaster, member of HCR Advisory Board

*Aida Frey*, thirteen-year-old National Park Service Junior Ranger: Her father was like a "stage mother" in that he kept asking me to interview her about being a junior ranger. He came to the interview and kept stopping her to remind her to tell different stories.

*John Buckley*, executive director, Adult & Child Therapy

*Robin Doeden & Margaret Miller*, McHenry County Community Foundation: After interviewing both of them about their foundation, I learned that HCR qualified to receive grants from the foundation. We applied and received $10,000 from them, and received the same amount in the following year.

*Dave Novalinski*, About Your Home Inspection: I learned so much about home inspection services that his company provided. I almost hired them to inspect my home. I know if I ever decide to sell the house, I definitely would bring him in to do the inspection report, assuming it shows that the house is in perfect shape.

*Bill Geheren,* Heritage Woods of Huntley: He is a member of the HCR executive board, the host of the show "Two Dudes and the Duchess," and, by appointment, HCR's Marketing Director

*Laurie Dayon,* director, "Girls on the Run"

*T. R. Kerth,* author, columnist, & musician

*Ed Pierce,* electrician and general handy man: I met Ed, when the handy man I'd been using moved to Texas. Ed is now my "go to" guy whenever I had a problem with the house and its contents. He's terrific and can fix almost anything.

*Jake Marino,* president, Huntley Historical Society

*David Hunter,* Green Room Productions, a local "improv" theater group

*Debra Quackenbush,* McHenry County Department of Health: I've been talking to them for about a year, trying to get them to start a monthly show, and it looks like we're finally going to do it. Instead of Debra Quackenbush, I'm working with Keri Zaleski.

*Scott Chamberlain & Dennis Ahrens,* Northern IL Fire Museum: After interviewing Scott, I learned that he was going to give up the presidency of the museum, so I talked him into joining HCR's staff, and he did.

*Herb Kelly,* Pencil & Palette Art Club of Sun City: He hosted the show, *Tennis Love* for quite a while. Then he started another new show *You Can Book It.* Eventually, he turned his tennis show over to another player, and now does only *You Can Book It.*

*Bernice Bakley,* Huntley Travel

*Elizabeth Kienzle,* School District 158 LIGHT Program

*John Scharres,* managing director, Woodstock Opera House

*Charles Sass,* mayor, Village of Huntley

*Dr. Gene Crume,* president, Judson University

*Harriet Blake*, professional performer-singer

*Williams Street Repertory Company*, the resident theater company at the Raue Center in Crystal Lake: They did a promo for their newest musical, bringing their director, three performers, and the music director with his keyboard for a great preview of the show.

*Steve Otten,* executive director, United Way of McHenry County

*Betty Kamps,* conductor, Sun City Encore Chamber Orchestra

*Martha Brenner,* concertmaster, Sun City Encore Chamber Orchestra

*Ray Thomas*, winner, Sun City Idol Contest, a great baritone and an interesting story to go with it.

*Cynthia O'Connor-Smith*, director, Lifestyles Sun City

*Anita Whalen*, director, Woodstock Mozart Festival: We became very friendly, and I tried to come up with ideas to promote Mozart and get more of an audience.

*Rick Atwater*, Northwest Community Counseling & DUI Services

*David Williams*, "Write On" Club, Sun City

*Laurie Bivona*, director of marketing, Pioneer Center

*Patrick Maynard*, president, Pioneer Center

*Donna Kassens*, JourneyCare, a fundraiser for a hospice organization

*Paddy McKevitt*, Bravehearts Therapeutic Riding & Educational Center

*Sal Nigro*, Huntley Book Warehouse

*Moe Ross*, founder, Miographies, a business that interviews people, writes biographies, and turns them into books

*Kelly Pokharel*, director, CASA

*Donna Lake*, Northern Illinois Food Bank

*Scott Neuman & Matt Nickelson*, Free Guitars for Future Stars

*Sarah Ponitz*, Senior Care Volunteer Network

*Ann Grenevich*, "Ruth Ann's Sweets Bakery"

*Deputy Aimee Knop*, McHenry County sheriff's office

*Dave Larson*, manager, Village of Huntley

*Victor Narusis*, business recruitment manager, Village of Huntley

*Dr. John Burkey*, superintendent, School District 158

*Mark Altmayer*, CFO, School District 158

*Thom Palmer*, Huntley Park District executive director, member of the HCR Advisory Board, our landlord, and a great friend of HCR

*Dr. Chad Binger*, Binger Chiropractic

*Priya Narthakii*, yoga instructor

*Scott Iddings*, Leggee Elementary principal, and *Dawn Bach*, Leggee kindergarten teacher

*Ben Holly*, trainer, Centegra Health Systems

*Rich Myers*, manager, Culvers Restaurant

*Dawn Ellison & Lonni Oldham*, Huntley Area Veterans Foundation

*Camille Paddock*, HHS student and founder of Cam's Dare to be Different

*Rick Hagerty*, host, *Radio Roots* show

*John Perkins*, chief, Huntley Police Department

*Ken Caudle*, chief, Huntley Fire Department

*Christine Jurs*, Advance Design Company

*Doug Cataldo*, Huntley Area Public Library

*Mike Willis*, entrepreneur

*Tim Nash*, commander, Huntley American Legion

*President*, Sun City Golf Club

*Kathy Poelker*, Windy City Voices: Kathy starts her show in the fall of 2016

*Patricia Hare*, author, *Why Seniors Should Write Their Memoirs*

*Dave Rosenfeldt*, CPA and host, *Financial Straight Talk* and *Access with Respect* shows

*Frank Novak*, director, Huntley Public Library

*Jeanine Hill-Soldaner*, artist and host, *Vet Net*

*Renee Swanson*, Sun City marketing/special events manager

*Linda Strohschein*, elder law attorney, host, *Protecting what Matters*, a show about elder law

*Jaki Berggrean*, ED McHenry Visitor's' Bureau

*Elaine Shaw*, author: She gave me copies of two of her books, and they are very good

*Joe Pesz*, McHenry County Youth Orchestra

*Stan "Tex" Banas*, Roadside History of Illinois

*Bill Jorgensen*, DeFiore Jorgensen Funeral and Cremation Home

# World Travels

I have always loved to travel. Before I got married, I discovered Youth hostels and went on some of their local trips. Much later in life, Al and I discovered Elderhostels, which we visited around the world. The program changed its name to the Road Scholar.

In 1979 or 1980, I went with a JCC (Jewish Community Center) group to Rancho La Puerta in northern Mexico, just across the border from San Diego. Rancho La Puerta was an all-vegan resort with beautiful scenery, hikes into the mountains, and daily exercise program. Right up my alley—no meat, lots of exercises, etc.

During the ten days, they had a handwriting analyst interpret our handwriting. Here's what she said about me: "Energetic, determined, proud, feels emotions deeply, holds emotions in check, could explode, likes to be with people, clear thinker, picky, quick study, likes good lively discussions, practical, high goals, discrete, adaptable, flexible, strong need of security, status quo." Am I?

At Rancho La Puerta, many of the women would sneak into town for a hamburger because they couldn't follow the vegan diet. All in all, a wonderful trip.

*Buenos dias, senora.* (Good day, miss.) *Como se llama?* (What's your name?) *No se.* (I don't know.) *Cual es?* (What is?) *Cuando costa?* (How much is it?) *Mi esposo* (my husband). *Mi casa* (my home). *Mi cumpleanos es el catorce de octubre.* (My birthday is October 14.) And a very important question: *Donde esta el bano?* (Where's the bathroom?), and a few more. My dream, my image, was to be able to speak Spanish, but so far I speak *muy poco* (very little).

After four years of high school Spanish, two weeks in an Elderhostel program at the Universidad in Cuernavaca Mexico, nighttime classes at the local community college, and later with Sun City's own Jerry Green, and many Rosetta Stone lessons on my computer, I'm still trying to get it. I know some people have an "ear" for languages, and I guess I don't, but I've always imagined myself communicating in Spanish anywhere, anytime.

When we were in Guatemala, I really wanted to talk to people. "My, what an adorable baby" or "How do I get to a drugstore?" It didn't matter. In high school, back in those long-ago days, the teacher never "spoke" the language. I received straight A's, but all I could do was to read and write; we never learned to speak. I've forgotten many words from that time, but amazingly, a lot stayed with me. Not so these days! After learning new phrases and words in our Sun City class, I find that a few hours later, I cannot remember them for the life of me.

A while back, I purchased a Berlitz "learn the language" package, which consisted of a workbook and several audiotapes, which I played in the car while I was driving. I found out that if I kept repeating and repeating a phrase, it finally stayed with me.

When we were at the airport in Buenos Aires last February and I couldn't find my luggage anywhere, one of these memorized phrases came back to me, *Busco mis maletas* (I can't find my luggage). The Argentinean baggage helpers looked up in astonishment, hustled, and found the missing pieces. What a thrill!

Once in Cuernavaca, I needed new flashlight batteries and found out from the hotel that ROBINSON'S DEPARTMENT STORE was where I would find them. Instead of taking a taxi (same word in Spanish), I got on a bus (autobus), and when I got off, I didn't know which way to go. I stopped an older woman on the street and asked, "Donde esta Robinson's?" She looked a little surprised, BUT she pointed to the corner building, and there it was. I politely said, "*Gracias*" and walked to the store.

Inside, I located the counter where I could purchase batteries. When the clerk spoke to me in Spanish, I didn't know what she was saying nor did I know the word for batteries, so I said "batteryas." She didn't understand me, so I pointed to the display behind the counter. She looked puzzled, and I said I "desired batteryas C." She nodded her head and repeated, "Sí" ("Yes"). This went on for a while. I kept saying

"C," and she would repeat, "Si." Finally, I just went behind the counter and showed her the ones I needed. It was kind of like the Abbott & Costello's "Who's on first" bit!

In a restaurant in Havana, Cuba, many years ago on our honeymoon, the only food item I knew was *arroz con pollo* (rice with chicken). Later, I identified *huevos* (eggs), *pan* (bread), *mantequilla* (butter), and many other foods, and I could read the menu board in the McDonald's in Guatemala.

Al and I loved to travel before the kids were born, later during their growing up years, and even later after they were all on their own.

When the boys were old enough to travel, we took them to Greenfield Village, Dearborn, MI; Williamsburg Village, Virginia; Florida; Indiana Sand Dunes; Minnesota; Wisconsin and the Dells; overnight boat trips on the Milwaukee Clipper across Lake Michigan to Ludington, MI; Colorado; Arizona; California; a cross-country auto trip from Chicago to San Francisco and down the coast to San Diego; and Canada.

Al and I collected flags from each country we visited, bought a display rack, and there it all was.

Here they are in alphabetical order, followed by little stories about our visits to some of these countries:

| | | |
|---|---|---|
| Bahamas | India | Scotland |
| Belgium | Israel | Singapore |
| Canada | Italy | Soviet Union (St. Petersburg) |
| Costa Rica | Jamaica | Sweden |
| Cuba | Japan | Switzerland |
| Cyprus | Lichtenstein | Thailand (Phuket) |
| Denmark | Luxembourg | Turkey |
| Djibouti | Malaysia | U. S. – Alaska, Hawaii, |
| England | Mexico | Virgin Islands |
| Finland | Netherlands | Vatican City |
| France | (Holland) | West Germany |
| Guatemala | Oman | |
| Haiti | Puerto Rico | |

*Flag display*

## ANTARCTICA

Al and I flew from Chicago to Santiago, Chile where we took a bus to the port of Valparaiso to board our ship, the MS Celebrity Infinity. While we were in Valparaiso, we left the ship to go into the town where I found a department store where I wanted to buy new pants for Al. We found a place and actually got into the right department. Nobody spoke English, but going through the racks, we found the pants we were looking for but had to have them shortened. In spite of my high school Spanish, they couldn't understand me so we couldn't make the connection and we left.

We sailed down the west coast of South America, stopping at Puerto Monte Chili, the Chilean Fjords, the Strait of Magellan and Punta Arenas until we reached the southernmost tip of the continent—Ushuaia, Argentina. We were across the bay from the entrance to the continent of Antarctica. I bought a souvenir tee shirt that said, in Spanish, *el fin del Mundo*—the end of the world.

Antarctica is a pristine wilderness area. Icebergs in all shapes and sizes. Ten-thousand-foot peaks rising out of the sea. Glaciers. Long summer days that end with brilliant colors as dusk finally turns back into daylight. Abundant wildlife. Penguin colonies with tens of thousands of breeding pairs. Albatross with 10- to 13-foot wingspans. Elephant, Weddell, crabeater, leopard, and fur seals. Humpback, minke, and Orca whales. And no human population. Other cruise ships would have actually taken us on a three-day voyage into Antarctica, but we chose not to do it because we would have had to leave our ship and fly later to another port to get back on our first ship. But we did see seals, huge icebergs, and millions and millions of penguins.

When we left Ushuaia, we completed going around the tip of South America and up the east coast, stopping at Cape Horn, Chile; Puerto Madryn, Argentina; Punta Del Este, Uruguay; Montevideo, Uruguay; Punto Arena, Argentina; and ending in Buenos Aires where we flew back to the United States. As you can see, we hopped from Chile to Uruguay to Argentina.

## AUSTRIA

As we drove around Europe, we found ourselves in Austria. We felt as if we were in *The Sound of Music*, especially the scene where Maria is on a hilltop, singing. It was truly magical. One evening, we had dinner in a restaurant in an old town where costumed waitresses served big steins of beer. Once, Al stood up in the aisle, threw his arms in the air, and said, "Isn't this great?" He hadn't seen a waitress carrying a large tray behind him, and he totally hit the tray, knocking everything to the floor. I pretended I didn't know what idiot had done it.

Another time, we were in Salzburg and saw a parade of people walking down the narrow ancient streets, singing, and we followed them into a nearby church where it turned out a wedding was about to take place. It was a custom in Austria to march with the wedding couple to the church. So there we were in the church, watching the wedding ceremony. When they passed a basket to collect money for the young couple, Al threw some American dollars in the basket. We wondered when they emptied the basket later, if they were surprised to see our cash. Austria was beautiful, friendly, and storybook-like. We wondered how these wonderful people had dealt with the whole Nazi occupation.

## BELGIUM

We spent only two days in Belgium and visited museums and art galleries. Belgium is famous for beer (over one thousand and one hundred varieties), chocolate, waffles, and french fries, so we had to try some of them. While we think of french fries having originated in France, experts on such things insist it was a Belgium invention. Godiva is one of most famous Belgian chocolates. Al and I enjoyed having dinner in one of the great restaurants in that country, and the locals taught us a lot about what to do and see there.

## MEXICO

We visited Ensenada, Cabo San Lucas, Puerto Vallarta, Acapulco, Mexico City, Cuernovaca, Tijuana, and many other places. We watched the boys diving off the cliffs, improved our Spanish at the Universidad, ate great Mexican food—not tacos and burritos—real gourmet food.

At some point, we discovered Elderhostel. This wonderful organization for older (elder) people handles trips all over the world. They offer great old hotels or inns, terrific guides, all at incredibly low prices covering everything except travel. We found these so-called "elders" terrific—adventurous, outgoing, and marvelous trip companions.

## AUSTRALIA/NEW ZEALAND

Our longest international Elderhostel trip started on October 22, 2002, lasting for three weeks, ending November 11, and traveling 8,192 miles to two foreign countries, New Zealand and Australia. We were so excited.

We flew from Chicago's O'Hare Airport on October 23 to Los Angeles and took another flight to Auckland, New Zealand, arriving on October 22. We lost a whole day! The trip from LA was about nineteen or twenty hours. We got to know our fellow passengers very well.

One Australian warned us that when we were in the Outback of Australia, there may be a tremendous amount of big, black flies and recommended we get mosquito net hats. He also told us that at this date in October, the flies shouldn't be as bad as they would have been in August and September. We did not purchase hats, and the flies were around but not too bad.

The Auckland airport exhibits decorations in bright, colorful Maori symbols. We learned that the Maori tribes are the indigenous people of New Zealand. We met the rest of our Elderhostel group and our group leader, Charles Morris, called "Chaz," not Chuck or any other nickname for Charles. He was a tall, very nice-looking man, and extremely knowledgeable and friendly, the perfect guide. There were about fifty people in our group, all from the United States. We were exhausted, so we went to our hotel and caught up on sleep.

The next day, we began our adventures in New Zealand. Chaz gave us some background on Auckland and New Zealand, generally. New Zealand consists of two main islands separated by a body of water named Cape Strait. Auckland was on the north island and started out as its capitol, but later they moved it to Wellington. We loved New Zealand: not only a beautiful country, great weather, but also wonderfully friendly people.

As part of our visit, we went to the Maori Arts & Crafts Institute and attended Maori cultural performances and villages. New Zealanders treat the Maoris very well, not the way the Australians treat their indigenous people, the Aboriginals; from what I observed, they treat them as we treat our Native Americans. They were wandering around, dirty, poorly dressed, and asking for money to buy whiskey. There was a movie called *Rabbit-Proof Fence* that showed how the settlers in

*Steering the boat in Auckland!*

1931 decided to take the aboriginal children away from their families and keep them in orphanage-type buildings to train them to be like the rest of the Australian natives.

We traveled on both the north and south islands and saw beautiful beaches (one entirely covered in black sand), geysers, waterfalls, the famous Blue Mountains, a geothermal valley with bubbling hot springs, and a volcanic valley where we actually stood on top of a volcano. We took a sailboat cruise

*Feeding the sheep*

on Auckland Harbor, and were in the Glow Worm Caves, which are famous for the great echoes you get when you shout out. Somebody in the group suggested that the whole group sing something, so we could experience this unusual echo, and everybody pointed to me because they knew I loved singing. I began singing *You Are My Sunshine*, and the whole crowd joined in. WOW! What an echo! After that, whenever the group wanted to have fun, we began singing that song. We had such a great time. I told Al if it weren't so far from our kids, I'd love to move there, and I was serious.

After spending about a week in wonderful New Zealand, we flew to Sydney, Australia, and began our second adventure. Except for this flight, most of our travel was on very comfortable buses. Every hotel we stayed at was terrific and the food was great. Here are some of the highlights of the trip.

Sydney was a great city to visit. We were booked into the beautiful Ibis Hotel right on Sydney Harbor. When we went down to eat, we found that Vegemite was a favorite Australian snack. I bought some and tasted it. It was like eating a cake of yeast, but I was told it's very healthy. I brought some home with me, and nobody liked it.

We toured the famous Sydney Opera House, and Al and I attended a dance performance that evening. The opera house is right on Sydney Harbor, and there was a huge bridge spanning the water. They asked us if we wanted to join our group going to the top to a walkway across the bridge. We said, "No, thanks" and watched others doing it.

One day, our group was going to a very famous beach, and Al signed up. Our son, Doug, was in town, participating in the Gay Games VI, an Olympic event held every four years in different cities around the world. Doug was on the international committee and had attended all the planning meetings, as he had done in South Africa, Germany, Ireland, France, and more. When Al left for the beach tour, I got into a cab to meet Doug at the beautiful, historic Queen Victoria Building (QVB) housing a large shopping mall. This was when the Gore/Bush election controversy was still fresh in people's minds. While I was in the cab, the driver, when he learned I was from the States, began talking about that election. "Don't you people know how to run an election?" That was an eye-opener for me. I hadn't realized that our election mess was known around the world. I told him that I didn't think we did and was actually ashamed of the whole situation.

Doug and I had a wonderful reunion and lunch. He gave me two VIP tickets to the opening ceremony of the games on the next day, and Al and I went. We had fantastic seats. Doug was in a huge marching band that played during the opening ceremonies, and, while in Australia, they played in several concerts.

The Gay Games made its first journey to the southern hemisphere in the new millennium. The games opened in this huge Aussie Stadium, and after the opening, used many, many venues for the different athletic events. There were eleven thousand athletes involved and one thousand one hundred cultural participants from more than seventy countries.

While in Sydney, we visited the site of the 2000 Olympics, did some shopping, and became familiar with the city.

After a couple of days, we left Sydney to begin our journey into the "wilds" of the continent. We got to Alice Springs, which was the "gateway" to the Outback, or the interior of the country. In Alice

Springs, I attended one of their weekly Rotary meetings. Having been a member of Rotary since my Centre East days, I thought it was great fun to experience a meeting so far from home. Although Rotarians around the world had a "men only" policy, everyone in attendance made me feel welcome. Incidentally, I had the same experience when Al and I were in Finland, and I went to a Rotary meeting. No women, and it was all in the Finnish language, but a very nice Finnish Rotarian translated everything to me.

We left Alice Springs and traveled into the Outback. Did you know that camels came into Australia early in its history because they not only could carry a lot of equipment, but they could travel long distances through the Australian desert with very little need for water? We visited a camel farm, and a couple of our group actually took camel rides.

The enormous ranches in the Outback are called cattle stations. Australian cowboys were everywhere. We stayed at these cattle stations and enjoyed a typical Aussie barbeque. It was huge and delicious. After eating dinner, when night fell, a professor of astronomy from the local college passed out flashlights and led us into an open field on the ranch. Thank goodness, we had those flashlights because it was pitch black. There he introduced us to the sky, which was totally different from the sky in the northern hemisphere. Where we were in the southern hemisphere, we were below the equator, and everything was turned around. Where was the Big Dipper?

While traveling through the Outback, we stayed overnight in different in bush camps, and at one of them, I picked up recipes for Bush Brownies and Damper, the bush-bread of Australia. Drovers (cowboys) baked damper in camp ovens buried in the hot ashes of their campfires, but if you don't want to build a campfire in your backyard, you can bake it in your kitchen oven. To eat damper, cut it into rustic chunky slices, spread a liberal amount of butter on it, and top with either jam, honey or pancake syrup. YUM! As the Aussies say, "You just got to have a cuppa with it." I got the recipe when we visited the Doramino bush camp. When I came home, I actually baked it and found out it was just our regular bread. I don't know why it's called Damper. Here is the recipe.

## Australian Damper Bread

4 cups self-raising flour
½ teaspoon salt
1-1/2 cups milk
Butter for greasing the pan
Extra flour for dusting the pan

### Directions

Sift the flour and salt into a bowl and make a well in the middle.
Pour in the milk and mix.
Grease the camp oven or round baking pan and dust with flour.
Place dough in the camp oven or pan.
Cut a cross in the top surface of dough.
Close lid of camp oven and bake in the hot ashes of your
campfire for about thirty minutes, or bake in preheated normal
kitchen oven for 30 minutes at 220° C (425° F).
Eat with a cup of tea, boiled in a billy (a metal or enamelware
pail or pot with a lid and wire bail —called also *billycan*).

We saw camels, visited a large wildlife park where we saw bats, giant gray and red kangaroos, dingoes, penguins, koala bears (not really bears but that's what the Aussies call them), wallabies, and kookaburras, known as the laughing bird from the song "Kookaburra sits on the old gum tree, merry, merry king of the bush is he, laugh kookaburra, laugh kookaburra, gay your life must be." They actually laugh. I learned that song when I was about twelve or thirteen in my first "go away" camp. We also saw giant kingfishers, huge termite mounds, and many, many weird insects.

We went to so many fantastic places in Australia, including a bubbling warm spring where we sat on hot rocks to "warm our buns" as Chas told us. My birthday stone is the opal, and I had decided that because they mine opals in Australia, I would buy one while we were there, and I did. It was a beautiful stone with the typical bluish colors, but even though they mine them there, the price was probably the same as in the United States. I love it and think of this trip every time I wear it.

One of the highlights of the trip was "Breakfast with the Birds." This event took place in a great wildlife park. We were on an outdoor patio, eating a full, delicious breakfast, listening to the jungle sounds and the music of the birds. These tropical birds swooped down and nibbled at toast and cakes that we gave them. They were clean and not bothersome at all. While in this tremendous park, we were in a couple of rain forests and went to see the famous Olgas Rocks.

The biggest highlight of it all was a visit to Ayers Rock, also known in the indigenous language as Uluru. It's one of Australia's most popular visitor sites. It's amazing. We traveled through this flat, desert-like country when, all of a sudden, we saw a huge red rock, and I mean huge. The natives treat it like a holy object, and no one has permission to climb it. They told us to be sure to see the sunrise over the rock. We had been staying in a hotel near this location, and the staff woke us very, very early in order to get on our bus and see the sunrise.

When we arrived at the viewing site, other tourist buses were also there. Our bus personnel had set up a beautiful breakfast at the site. It was still dark outside. When the sun was due to rise, it began raining and got very cloudy. We ate the breakfast but never saw the sunrise. All of this was on the western coast of the continent.

We next were in the northern territory at the famous Great Barrier Reef. This reef is one of the World Heritage Sites. I learned there are 1,031 sites all over the world. A place is designated a World Heritage because of its unusual cultural or natural significance, and is listed by UNESCO. The Great Barrier Reef is listed; it's the equivalent of 1,243 miles and can be seen from space.

We took a glass-bottom boat tour because the waters were so clear, we could see to the bottom. Unfortunately, there had been a storm recently, and the sand was so stirred up we couldn't see anything. I guess I'll have to go back to Australia so I can see a sunrise at Uluru and see to the bottom of the ocean at the Great Barrier Reef. We stayed at the reef in the nearby city of Cairns. This whole area is very tropical; as we traveled north in Australia, it became very Florida-like as we approached the equator.

Among our traveling companions was a retired doctor, (Jean) who had several cameras, even an underwater one. After we returned home, she sent copies of all the pictures she had taken. Another fellow traveler, Ralph Conway, a retired architect and wonderful artist, sketched eleven

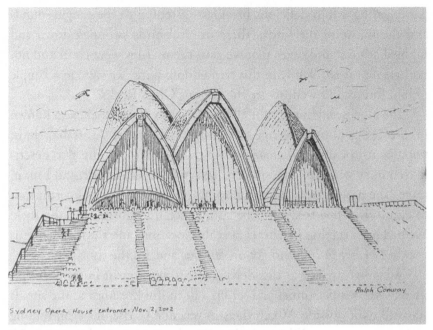

*Sydney Opera House by Ralph Conway, fellow Elderhosteler*

places we had visited. After we got home, he sent them to me. I framed them and included one of them in my memoirs.

I'm sure Al would agree with me that this Elderhostel tour of New Zealand and Australia was absolutely one of the best travel adventures we ever took.

## BAHAMAS

When we first started cruising, we began with a short cruise to the Bahamas, which is actually a small separate country. The Bahamas, consisting of seven hundred islands in the Atlantic Ocean and covering over 180,000 square miles of ocean, is part of a larger island chain that it shares with the Turks and Caicos Islands. We visited some of these smaller islands, but our main visit was to Nassau, the capitol. A couple of things stand out in my memory. Al had some kind of investment in Nassau, so when we docked there, he walked down the gangplank in shorts, white socks, black leather oxfords, and carrying a briefcase. And another time, when we were visiting one of the very small islands, we passed a restaurant that advertised that they served bagels. At the time, bagels were kind of an exotic food, found mainly in New York and Chicago. How did they get out here?

## CANADA

We visited Canada a number of times. I was there before I married Al. I took a train from Chicago to Winnipeg, continued west to Calgary, known as the "gateway to the Rockies." It was my first time in the mountains, and I discovered that this train had added an open car, no roof, and when I went onto it, I was in awe of the beauty of the mountains. From Calgary, we continued west to Vancouver, British Columbia, one of the largest Canadian cities. I loved that city and Canada, in general. Vancouver consistently receives the designation as one of the top five worldwide cities for livability and quality of life. One of its tourist sites is the neighborhood called Gastown with its famous Steam Clock.

Steam provides heat for Vancouver, and they built the clock over a steam grate to prevent street people from sleeping over it in cold weather. Instead of bells chiming the hour, it blows a steam whistle. Al and I returned to Vancouver another time when we flew there to board a cruise ship to Alaska.

Across the bay (Victoria Strait) is Victoria Island. I toured this beautiful island but could not enjoy the famous high tea at the Empress Hotel. Unfortunately, one must make reservations at least two weeks in advance. Oh, well. I had planned to take a ship from Vancouver to Alaska, but I lost some luggage and by the time I recovered it, I had missed that cruise. I did visit Banff National Park and stayed at a great hotel at Lake Louise. It was a gorgeous lake, and one day I took a horseback tour with a group up into the mountains around Lake Louise.

Other Canadian trips include the Canadian World's Fair in Montreal in the summer of 1968. We went with all four boys: Jim was sixteen, Doug was fifteen, Sandy was eleven, and Marty four-and-a-half. We had a wonderful time at the fair and then drove to Quebec. Al took the three older boys on a tour highlighting a famous battle, but because Marty was so young, he and I stayed in Quebec and visited the French Quarter. While walking around, Marty got thirsty, so we went into a restaurant and asked for a glass of water. They didn't understand our English; it turned out that glass in French (*glace*) means ice, and that's what they gave us!

Another time, I attended a booking conference in Ottawa, the capitol of Canada. When I arrived, my luggage was missing, so I had to attend opening parties, dinners, etc., in my traveling clothes and snow boots until they found my luggage. I visited the Parliament and saw Santa Claus, who was dressed in green instead of the iconic red.

## COSTA RICA

We were on another cruise that left San Diego on its way to the Panama Canal and ended in Boca Raton, Florida. Doug happened to be in San Diego, and we stayed with him for a couple of nights and then began the cruise. Ports along the way included Ensenada, Cabo San Lucas, Puerto Vallarta, and Acapulco. One of the sights we saw in Acapulco was cliff diving by Mexican boys between narrow walls. It really was thrilling.

One very early morning, our ship was about to enter the Panama Canal from the Pacific Ocean to the Atlantic, and the captain woke us all up through the ship's speakers to announce that we were about to begin the transverse of the canal. It was about 5:00 a.m. We quickly dressed and went out on deck. There the ship had laid out a simple breakfast of juice, coffee, and bread/rolls. It was great.

The Panama Canal is "one of the seven wonders of the world." It is forty-eight miles long, takes twenty to thirty hours to go through, and has two lanes. A third wider lane, to accommodate today's larger ships, is under construction and is due to open in 2016.

We docked in Costa Rica and joined another couple, renting a taxi, which we thought would be better than signing up for a bus tour. Unfortunately, the driver spoke practically no English, so I attempted, in my "pidgin' Spanish" to tell him what we'd like to see. I guess he didn't really understand me, so we drove around the countryside and then returned to the ship.

## CYPRUS

When we visited Turkey, we also visited Cyprus, a large island in the Mediterranean. Cyprus was partitioned, one into the Republic of

Cyprus and the other into the Turkish Republic of Northern Cyprus, recognized only by Turkey. When the Republic of Cyprus joined the European Union, they declared the Turkish Republic of Northern Cyprus illegal. The dispute has not been resolved, despite many suggested solutions. We met Cypriots who cried at the wall separating the two partitions, saying that part of their family was on one side and the rest on the other side, and they couldn't see or visit each other.

## CUBA

We spent a week in Havana, Cuba, on our honeymoon in 1951. We originally drove to Miami Beach, Florida, but it was raining every day, so we drove south to Key West and flew on Cuban Airways to Havana where the sun was shining. This was in 1951 when Batista was in charge. Cuba was booming with tourists, casinos, music, and fun. We checked into a beautiful hotel and had a wonderful time. One night, we went to a Cuban restaurant and, with my limited Spanish, I recognized only arroz con pollo (rice with chicken), so that is what we had.

## DENMARK

Al's cousin, Jack Litwin, was living in Sweden, working at a lab in Copenhagen. He first moved to Denmark when he received his PhD in Microbiology from the University of Chicago and later switched to another lab in Stockholm, Sweden. In 1988 we decided to visit him in Stockholm. He had married and had a daughter, but his wife had died and his grown-up daughter lived in Iceland. We flew to Copenhagen where Jack met us.

On our first day, at breakfast, Jack offered us a glass of whiskey. Legal drinking starts at the young age of sixteen and the use of tobacco at eighteen. Denmark is a monarchy. I was surprised to learn that the Danes, Swedes, and Norwegians do not like each other and are very competitive. I had assumed all three of these Scandinavian countries were friendly toward each other.

Jack loved classical music, art, dance, and literature, and was very surprised when we had asked him if he could get us tickets to the Chicago Bears/Minnesota Vikings pre-season game in Gothenburg. He couldn't understand that we would want to spend time watching football instead of visiting their museums, et al. He did get us the tickets, though, and we all went to the game.

That evening, as we wandered through the town, we passed a closed shop, which had a Niles North jacket in the window. We always wondered how it got there. If the store had been open, we would have gone in and asked the owners.

## FINLAND

We took the Silja line ship from Sweden to Helsinki, Finland, where we spent a few days. Helsinki was a beautiful city and very friendly. We ate in a restaurant where they had a huge stuffed bear at the entrance. I went to a Rotary meeting, and because Rotary did not allow women to join, I was the only female at the meeting. The U.S. Rotary had just changed from a "no women" policy, but that hadn't happened yet in Europe and especially Finland. I sat next to a man who spoke English, and he translated from Finnish to English so I could follow what was happening. When I had to go to the bathroom, not being able to translate signage on the doors, I walked into the men's room.

# *Marty's Memories of This Trip*

Jack took us to some of the famous spots in Copenhagen, Denmark, like the Little Mermaid, a bronze statue by Edvard Eriksen, depicting a mermaid. The sculpture, which is 4.1 feet tall and weighs 385 pounds, sits on a rock by the waterside at the Langelinie promenade. Based on the fairy tale of the same name by Danish author Hans Christian Andersen, the small and unimposing statue is a Copenhagen icon and has been a major tourist attraction since 1913. In recent decades, it also has become a popular target for defacement by vandals and political activists.

We also toured Stockholm with Jack and saw all the touristy places. *Vasa* is a Swedish warship built between 1626 and 1628. It foundered and sank after sailing about 1,400 yards on her maiden voyage on August 10, 1628. She fell into obscurity after most of her valuable bronze cannons were salvaged in the seventeenth century until she was located again in the late 1950s in a busy shipping lane just outside the Stockholm harbor. Salvaged with a largely intact hull in 1961, they housed her in a temporary museum called *Wasavarvet* (The Wasa Shipyard) until 1988 and then moved her to the Vasa Museum in Stockholm. The ship is one of Sweden's most popular tourist attractions; more than twenty-nine million visitors have seen it since 1961. Since her recovery, *Vasa* is a widely recognized symbol of the Swedish "great power period" and is today a *de facto* standard in the media and among Swedes for evaluating the historical importance of shipwrecks.

I was around twenty-four when we saw the Bears play the Minnesota Vikings in Gothenburg. We went to the stadium the day before the game and got down on the field to take some pictures. As I recall, the Bears won that preseason game. CBS was broadcasting it, and Irv Cross, one of the announcers, walked right by us as he was going to the press box, and I shook his hand. Terry Bradshaw, another one of the game announcers, acknowledged us Americans from the press box as we were chanting his name. During the game, I taught the game to some locals who were sitting next to me, although they seemed to know a lot about it. We also went down to the players' entrance and stood near some of the Bears before they took the field.

That evening, there was a parade of classic U.S. cars from the 50s on the main street. I also remember the store of American memorabilia including a letterman's jacket from Niles North in the window!

One of the best things about that trip was the Swedes did not recognize the players, so they were able to walk around. We went to their hotel and saw Mike Tomczak, Cap Boso, Al Harris, and Dick Butkus (one of the broadcasters). Butkus was rather grumpy when we said hi to him.

We took a boat cruise down the river in Gothenburg, and Jerry Burns, the coach of the Vikings, was on it with us. Because the river was so high and the bridges so low, we all had to get down on the floor of the boat while we went under them or we would have hit our heads!

We seemed to eat all the time. Jack would suggest we get a coffee or something, and then we'd always get some kind of dessert or other food as well.

We took the Silja line ship from Sweden to Helsinki, Finland, where we spent a few days. Helsinki was a beautiful city and very friendly. In Helsinki, I remember that church carved into the rocks.

After visiting Helsinki, we took another ship, and I remember Dad lost his wallet. They paged him over the PA system on the ship once someone turned it in. I remember going on the deck that night and was amazed at how completely dark it was; only the sound of the ship traveling on the Baltic Sea could be heard.

I remember in St. Petersburg, USSR, it was still daylight at 9:45 p.m. This was in 1988, only three years before the fall of the Soviet Union, and I remember how rundown a lot of the buildings looked compared to 1984 when I had gone there as a student at the University of Wisconsin.

Overall, a great trip with many great memories!

## ISRAEL

They say everyone should go to Israel at least once in their life, especially if they're Jewish. Well, Al and I did it by way of a cruise. One of the stops was Haifa, so we arranged with the ship's captain to leave the ship in that port and return two days later. Al's cousin, Jack Litwin, and his wife Lea, lived in Israel. He was the son of Al's Aunt Fay. She had two sons: David, who graduated from the Goodman Theater School and became a professional actor; and Jack, who received his doctorate from the University of Chicago and was a microbiologist. When Al had been a student in graduate school at Northwestern University, he lived for a time with Aunt Fay and her two boys. Jack was about ten years old, and Al was about twenty.

We had contacted Jack and Lea and told them our plans and the dates we'd be landing in Haifa. They lived in the town of Nahariyya and said they'd drive to Haifa to meet us. It was really wonderful seeing them again. The last time we had seen them was in 1999 when they came to the United States and asked if we would join them at the Grand Canyon in Arizona. We did and had a great time.

We drove to Tel Aviv, stopping at Caesarea, an ancient, historic city. We visited the Roman open amphitheater and the ruins of the Roman port. It was very deserted, but it was a beautiful day and we enjoyed it. I actually walked on the stage of the amphitheater.

When we arrived in Tel Aviv, we went to eat in a restaurant in Jaffa. We learned that Jaffa had been a separate town but after its annexation to Tel Aviv, it became a kind of suburb. We checked into the Savoy Hotel across the street from a beautiful beach. I later learned that a few years earlier, there had been a terrible terrorist attack on that hotel by a Palestinian commando group which had come in from the sea and killed eight tourists. The hotel was supposed to have four stars, but it was quite run down; we learned that when we went into our rooms. There was a serious leak in our bathroom, and it was quite flooded. It took some time for the hotel personnel to fix it.

That evening, we drove to a Tel Aviv suburb to visit my daughter-in-law's mother, Hanna Schlesinger, who lived in a protected housing complex. She had a very nice studio apartment and felt very satisfied with her life there. She used to live in Morton Grove after escaping to Israel from Germany as a child in the 1930s. After visiting her, we returned to our hotel and went to sleep.

The next morning, we walked to a nearby hotel for breakfast. The restaurant had a beautiful outdoor terrace with a splendid view of the promenade and the sea. After breakfast, we drove to Jerusalem, checked into Hotel Moriah, and then picked up a friend of Jack and Lea's named Lotte. She had been a tourist guide who specialized in the sites of Jerusalem, the perfect person to show us around the city. We took a detailed tour of the old town, including the Wailing Wall and the El Aqsa mosque. At that time, there was no problem letting tourists go into the mosque, but we had to leave our shoes and purses or bags outside. Muslim employees were the guards, but when we came out, my purse was not where I had left it. Fortunately, my passport was not in the purse, but everything else was gone. When Al tried to put his shoes back on, he lost his balance and fell, hitting his head on the wall of the mosque. He was bleeding quite a bit, and Lotte suggested we go to the Hadassah Hospital's emergency room. Al refused. Lotte had been a nurse before becoming a tourist guide, so she helped him to her apartment and dressed the wound. I don't remember if we reported all of that to the police or not, but I never did get my purse back. I hadn't lost much, so we weren't very upset. We decided that we would enjoy this visit no matter what happened.

After Al had recovered, we ate at a YMCA in a typical British colonial building, which had an excellent restaurant. That evening, we went to see folk dances; Al was very upset because there were no Palestinian dances, and that was what he particularly wanted to see. The show was quite mediocre, so we left before the end.

The next morning, after checking out, we had a huge Israeli breakfast. It was a very special meal with herring, all kinds of cheeses, breads, eggs, several salads, fruit, yogurt, cakes, coffee, and a variety of drinks. Then they drove us back to Haifa where we said our thanks and goodbyes. The whole experience was short but really remarkable.

# Diary of 30-Day World Cruise
## On Board The Renaissance 2

**November 6-7, 2000**

We flew from O'Hare to New York's LaGuardia Airport, intending to connect with Sabena Airlines, only to learn that the flight was overbooked. Our plan was to leave on Swissair. To compensate us for our troubles, they gave us $50 certificates to use at the airport restaurant—the Skyview—and $120 in Swiss Francs to be used in the duty-free shops. We were hungry, had about two hours to kill, went to the Skyview, and had a great buffet.

We landed in Zurich on time and had to wait for another couple of hours for the connecting flight to Athens. We finally boarded and ended up in Athens totally exhausted. Renaissance people met us, and, after going through customs, we boarded a bus, which took us to the ship. The ship was the same one we had been on about a year and a half earlier, so it was a little bit like coming home.

We had a beautiful cabin (#7086) on the seventh deck with its own balcony. When we checked into our stateroom, there was a huge basket of fresh fruit on the table, and we thought the cruise line had sent it. But after looking it over, we found a card. Doug had sent it!!!

We were so tired, we fell asleep immediately, and I woke up when the phone began ringing. It was Al. He called me to say the buffet would stop serving in a half an hour. I quickly dressed in my travel outfit, and we had a late dinner. Stuffed cabbage was on the menu, so it was worth it. We ate on the outside deck, went to the library, picked up some books, and went to the new Internet Cafe. Al left me there, and once the manager of the cafe had entered the passenger info into his computer, I was free to send an e-mail. Unfortunately, I had left everyone's e-mail address in the room and had memorized only Doug's. I wrote him an e-mail and asked that he call the rest of his brothers to let them know we made it on the ship. The letter ended up costing around $12.

The port for Athens is Piraeus. The currency is the Greek drachma. The approximate conversion was $1.00 U.S. = 403 drachma. The weather forecast for November 7 and 8 was "sunny, pleasant & breezy" with a high of 80F, low 63F. Distance to Rhodes is 371 nautical miles.

**Days 2, 3**

Many passengers took sightseeing tours of Athens, but we didn't because we had been here before and had seen the Parthenon, Acropolis, etc. We stayed on board, went into the swimming pool and whirlpool, registered in the new Internet Café, and sent another e-mail to Doug and asked him to call the rest of the Litwin's and tell them about the e-mail. Besides the Internet Café, there is an IBM unit in the library. I'm using it right now with WordPerfect 9. It's very similar to the Mac Word except there are some commands that are different. (I just found a book on the library shelves for WordPerfect 8, so I will try to figure out how to insert, correct, etc.)

The food is truly terrific and there is so much of it. Service is exceptionally good, and the place is extremely clean and comfortable. Mostly we did a lot of catch-up sleeping.

Rhodes weather was "pleasant with sunshine," high 75F, low 63F. While on Rhodes, besides taking pictures, we bought a pillow cover for Karin (a rooster design); the woman who was at a loom weaving rugs and other pillow covers did not speak English, and when Al asked the cost, all she could say was "5,000 drachmas." This became a source of great amusement to us because she kept repeating that phrase.

We had been to Rhodes before, but we walked into the Old Town (a walled city). It was another beautiful day of 70+ degrees with brilliant sunshine. The sun god Helios, as the story goes, chose Rhodes and bestowed upon the island the gift of perpetual sunshine.

Rhodes is also associated with the Colossus of Rhodes, one of the Seven Wonders of the Ancient World. Built in 305BC to honor the sun god, the Colossus was a huge bronze statue standing over 100 feet tall. Nothing remains of the statue itself, and even its exact position is unknown. In the fourteenth century, the Knights of St. John occupied the island. That was when Muslims took control of the Holy Land, and the Knights, forced to leave, came to Rhodes. They ruled for two hundred years and built a fortified town where the Old Town still stands; it is the largest inhabited medieval fortification in the world.

The Ottoman Turks took over in 1522 and destroyed much of the medieval architecture, and converted many churches to mosques and built several new mosques. In 1912 the Italians took over and began huge architectural restoration projects. The Germans took control in 1943, and finally, in 1945 the Allies liberated Rhodes, and the Greek flag was hoisted in 1948.

We had signed up for an all-day tour for when we arrived in Port Said, Egypt. We were at sea all day. The tour would take us by motorized convoy to the pyramids and The Great Sphinx. The convoy would have armed police in front, rear, and sides, and we had the assurance of the ship's tour director that we would be safe. The only warning we received was not to crawl into the pyramid if we were claustrophobic (and believe me, I do not intend trying it). We also signed up for a tour in Sharm el Sheikh. We would pass through the Suez Canal.

## November 11, 2000

We arrived in Port Said, Egypt, having traveled from Rhodes, Greece, across the Mediterranean and to the entrance of the Suez Canal. So far, the trip has been uneventful, the weather perfect, as is the ship's service, food, etc. When we woke up, it was so foggy that we couldn't see the water from our balcony.

Some facts: 95 percent of Egypt's population is Muslim. Egypt is one of the world's oldest continuous civilizations; sometime around 2925 BC, a king named Menes united Upper and Lower Egypt (thus the Menes hotel name). The currency in Egypt is the Egyptian pound, and the approximate conversation factor was $1.00 U.S. = 3.7 EGP.

We went on the all-day tour to the pyramids, the sphinx, and the Egyptian Museum. Actually, it was foggy but it cleared up, the sun came out, and it was beautiful. We boarded one of the eight tour buses at 7:30 a.m. Each bus held about forty people. The buses, air-conditioned and very comfortable, traveled convoy fashion for our safety with soldiers riding in front and hack. The trip, which took three hours, took us to Cairo. Just outside of the city were the pyramids. We crossed the Nile River several times.

(By the way, when we first boarded R2, we turned in our passports to the purser and received a guest card, which opened our stateroom door, acted as a charge card for purchases, casino playing, etc. But we were told that in Egypt we would have our passports returned to us because the Egyptian authorities would have to stamp them when we exited the ship and that we should keep our passports with us all the time we were in Egypt.)

One thing we had noticed as we rode the bus up to Cairo was the large number (hundreds) of half-finished buildings. They looked like tenements. Our guide told us that the farmers in the area began the construction of these buildings for their children to finish when they were ready to move out of their parents' home when they married. It seems that children stay with their parents until they get married, no matter what their age.

When we arrived at the pyramids, it was quite a sight. There were three pyramids, the largest known as the Great Pyramid, which took more than two million blocks of stone to construct. The second pyramid, Chephren, is smaller than the first, but because it stands on slightly higher ground, it appears as tall as the Great Pyramid. Then there is the 31d or smallest pyramid, which is much smaller than the other two, and it reopened to the public after several years of refurbishment. The lower part of it still contains part of the original granite slab covering. We could have crawled into this opening but we didn't. The purpose of pyramids was to house the mummified bodies of the pharaohs.

The sphinx is just off to the side. This monumental half-lion, half-man has "presented a mystery to scholars and scientists for centuries." No one knows exactly when or why the Egyptians built it. We took a number of pictures around the pyramids and the sphinx.

We received warnings that as soon as we left the ship, hawkers of all types of merchandise would surround us. They don't take "no" for an answer. We were to just keep looking ahead and ignore them. However, we did buy postcards and a raffia camel from them. If they hadn't been so pushy, I think I could have bought a lot more. I'm sure we will see duplicates of this type of selling later on in Egypt and wherever

*Al at the pyramids*

we go. They attempt to sell an item for $10, then $7, then $5, and then $2 is usually the settled price if you couldn't help but relent. Already some folks have purchased so much, you wonder how they'll get it all home. Around the pyramids, some of the hawkers sold camel rides or "take your picture on a camel – $1 .00"!

The pyramids are in the desert, and as we looked around, I felt we were back in the days of the Bible. Men in turbans rode donkeys (*We Three Kings of Orient Are*), swift riders were on horseback or on camels, and all wore the *galabaya* (long robe). The women also wear them and cover their heads, except in Egypt, it is by personal choice and not required by law as it is in Saudi Arabia, Iran, etc. Many wore western clothing.

## November 12, 2000

We went through the Suez Canal, which is 121 miles long. It connects three lakes and has no locks because the water levels of the Gulf of Suez and the Mediterranean Sea are the same. The majority of the canal is one-lane only. The British commanded the canal from 1936 until 1954, and in 1956, all British troops departed, and Egypt took over the British installation. At the end of the canal, we were in the Gulf of Suez and then the Red Sea. The Red Sea color resulted from the dying off blue green algae, which imparts a reddish color to the water.

Following the desert trek, we had lunch at the Mena Hotel, built for a French queen around 1902. It is magnificent with its crystal, marble, and beautiful furnishings. It has an Indian feeling about it in the shape of its doors and windows. The huge buffet lunch included wine, Egyptian beer, soft drinks, coffee, and tea.

We boarded the bus and went to the Egyptian Museum. Here we viewed the mummified remains of pharaohs from several different dynasties. Also there was an entire King Tut area where we saw the artifacts taken from his tomb, which was uncovered in 1922. This same exhibit was in Chicago several years ago. We were quite tired by this time but felt re-charged at this exhibit. It was fascinating. We arrived back at the ship around 8:00 p.m.

A couple from Montreal, Alex and Luiza, had gone into the local village and bought some lovely pieces of 18K gold jewelry for about half the price of what it was in Cairo. I became involved in a bit of a switch-scam from a local jewelry shop. I know better than to let myself rush into something, but I let it happen. I wanted them to personalize the piece that I had purchased. They would then deliver it to me at the museum just before the bus left to return to the ship. They substituted a less-valuable piece. Well, that won't happen to me again.

The port of Sharm el Sheikh is at the southernmost tip of Egypt. Our trip into the Sinai desert was an all-day trip, a three-hour bus ride each way to the Valley of the Kings. I was primarily interested in visiting St. Catherine's monastery at the top of Mt. Sinai, but they cancelled that part of the trip. The sail through the Suez Canal from Port Said to here had been quite interesting. (Others told us that the Panama Canal is much narrower and advised us that if we took that trip in the future to be sure the schedule is for a daytime transit. The rates are lower at night, but the daytime traverse is most interesting. Maybe someday.)

Many of our fellow travelers were quite dissatisfied on this R2 ship. There was a lot of grumbling and asking one another if they were satisfied. The ship has an "air" about it; lack of hospitality at the front desk. Because of the itinerary switch, many are out of pocket for buying the required visas by the previously scheduled ports. Some speculation surfaced that the cruise line was growing too fast and that possibly they were having financial difficulty. Many of us have sailed the Renaissance ships before and knew the difference.

## November 13, 2000

We arrived at the port of Safaga on the Red Sea after going through the Suez Canal the previous night. Our tour director instructed us to carry our passports with us at all four Egyptian ports and to return our passports to the purser when we left Safaga, Egypt, our last port.

We signed up for a bus tour to Luxor via the desert and agricultural roads. The bus was very comfortable, with good air conditioning and even its own toilet. The bus ride took around three hours, and even though we had brought along books and magazines, we dozed on and off. Our young tour guide, Sahar (Sahara without the "a"), was excellent and very knowledgeable. It seems the tour guides attend what they call "Tourist University."

Along the way, after passing through long desert stretches, we arrived at the agricultural part of Egypt. There were fields of cabbage, tomatoes, and other vegetables. The scenes from the bus were like scenes from the Bible. People dressed in the traditional galabaya, the long frock that both men and women wear. The women primarily wear black and cover their heads with black scarves. The Bedouin women bring the scarves around their heads and cover the lower half of their faces, probably to keep the sand out and to conform to customs.

The scene that we saw everywhere was men wearing turbans and sitting astride donkeys. They were not wearing some costume to show off for the tourists. This was their way of life. Farming was all hands-on and involved men, women, and children. Children were required to attend public school until the age of twelve. Their houses are mostly shacks made out of mud-bricks. The mud insulates the interiors from the heat and cold. However, people everywhere had smiling, friendly faces. We had to go through armed checkpoints and towers with soldiers in them. We had security around our bus convoy, both in front and back. There were ten buses in our convoy.

We arrived at the Temple of Karnak, which has the tombs of over thirteen centuries of successive pharaohs. The area is comprised of more than a hundred acres of majestic pylons, halls, and sacred temples. The hieroglyphics on the walls tell the story of the Egyptian belief in the after-life. Only the pharaohs' tombs are here.

Following about an hour at Karnak, we boarded the bus for a buffet lunch at the Sonest Luxor Hotel. It seemed people from all the buses from the Renaissance were having lunch there. The food was delicious, but they gave us only fifty minutes to get the food, eat it, and then get back on the bus. I ate my first persimmon here. It looked like an orange/red tomato, but it was delicious.

We were on the east bank of the Nile before, but after lunch, we went to the west bank to visit the Valley of the Kings, including the tomb of King Tutankhamun, the boy pharaoh, who died or was the victim of murder at the age of eighteen. (In the news, before we left for this trip, there had been a story about how scientists were doing DNA tests on the King Tut body. I asked our guide about this, and she said they were but she didn't know how they were going about it.) We did not see the actual remains but instead looked upon a sarcophagus. Webster's dictionary says it is a "stone coffin, bearing sculpture and inscriptions, often displayed as a monument."

Next was a short photo stop at the Temple of Queen Hatshipsut, followed by another short photo stop at the Colossi of Memnon facing the Nile. It was beginning to get dark, but we proceeded to the east bank of the Nile again to visit the Temple of Luxor, built over several centuries by Pharaohs Amenophis III, Tutankhamun, Ramses II, and Alexander the Great. Dramatic lighting of the pylons, columns, and walls made it a spectacular scene. There was, for example, an avenue of sphinxes linking it with the Karnak Temple. It is very fascinating. I'd like to come back again.

We returned to the ship around 10:00 p.m., and they had kept open the Panorama buffet until 11:00 p.m. so we could get dinner. After that monstrous buffet in Luxor, all I wanted were some veggies, fruit, and a roll. Al had bought a galabaya for himself and later one for me, and he wanted to wear his around the ship to judge people's reactions. I've concluded that there is a lot of "ham" in him.

## November 14, 2000

Today we had signed up for the Desert Safari, which left the ship at 9:00 a.m. and returned around 5:30 p.m. We boarded 4x4 vehicles, six to a vehicle and twenty vehicles in our convoy. The seating was very uncomfortable on side-facing benches. In order to get in, we had to climb up a very high step and crawl in. This was very difficult for just about all of us.

We drove out of Sharm el Sheikh where our ship had docked and traveled on a dusty road for miles. Each time, we had to stop and get out of the van and then re-enter later. The stops included a view of some ancient wall writings, box lunch (prepared by the ship), and another stop at a wadi (a gulley). For lunch, we sat either in a Bedouin tent or on mats on the sand. We drank Coke and afterward, a Bedouin woman made pita on a flat metal plate over a fire. She put rolls of dough on the metal plate and patted them down into thin circles. It was very tasty, except later, she cleaned her hands by digging into the sand around her. We also had mint tea, which was very sweet and good. The trip had been long and boring, and by the time we returned to the ship, the only thing we wanted to do was to crawl into bed and snooze. We left a call for 8:00 p.m., got up, and ate a late dinner in the Panorama buffet.

Tomorrow's port is Djibouti, North Africa, a distance of 1,081 nautical miles. The currency is $1.00US = 174DJF. Weather forecast: is for sun and clouds, high 88F, low 75F. It seems there will not be much to see or shop, but, regardless, the ship could not put into port unless every traveler had had a yellow fever inoculation. I asked to see documentation of that request but did not get anywhere with that from the medical office or the front office desk. The ship planned to refuel in Djibouti. In the interior of Africa, yellow fever is a virus spread through unclean water and by fly or mosquito bites.

## November 17, 2000

This is the third day we have been at sea—the Red Sea. Tomorrow, Sunday, we enter Djibouti, Djibouti (East Africa). A shuttle can take us to the Camel Market (shopping), but that's all we've been told. I understand that this is the first time this ship has traveled this route. It was a way for Renaissance to get the ship to Singapore where they'll run fourteen-day trips between Singapore and Hong Kong. Many people on this ship will remain on the ship after Singapore and travel to Vietnam.

We, as well as others, never bought a visa for Oman, and it turns out that the ship cannot get into the port unless everyone on board has an Oman visa. The ship is making us all get a visa for $90 each; there is much grumbling about this development. For the past two days (and also today), we spent most of the day sunning, eating, and reading. They have Bingo games and other activities, but we have not participated in most of them. My favorite place is the terrific library onboard. We met all kinds of people on board—lawyers, bankers, actors (community), doctors, teachers, etc.—people who have traveled a lot and love the adventure of unusual places.

Yesterday, I had bought some sandals, shirt, and shorts, and arranged for a personal consultant to prescribe an exercise program for my age. Of course, they have a great fitness center onboard. I also sent e-mails to Doug, Jim, Sandy, and Marty, but we received a frantic fax from Jim wondering where we were. We finally called him at work, and it turned out he had not received any of our e-mails.

## November 18, 2000

Here we are in Djibouti, Djibouti, East Africa. The heat and humidity are extremely high, and there are flies everywhere, really aggressive flies. (I almost swallowed one just standing on the dock.) Al wanted to go by taxi into the town, about a seven-minute ride ($5.00 each way divided by four people). I really didn't want to go after listening to the complaints from the people returning from their trip to town. The ship had arranged a shuttle bus for $59.99 per person, and those people, in particular, were the unhappiest as they returned by cab. Interesting story was that a couple was negotiating to purchase an ostrich egg and got the price down to $10 (by the way, although the currency here is the franc, they love to take American money). They gave the vendor a $10 bill, but he would not take it because he wanted one of our new bills.

At 2:00 p.m., we embarked to Oman, a three-day trip at sea. Even though many people (including us) had not purchased visas for Oman because we did not intend on going ashore, the cruise line said they had made arrangements for a purchase of visas for all of us who hadn't bought one. Shalala, Oman currency is $1.00 U.S. = 0.380 Rial. Onboard staff reminded us that all women must cover their heads to enter Job's tomb.

Following Oman, we will set sail for Mumbai (Bombay), India, a distance of 1,083 nautical miles. We crossed the Arabian Sea for three days, and the seas were calm, the weather sunny with a high of 87F and a low of 66F. PERFECT!!! After Bombay, India, plus other stops in India, we would go on to Thailand, Malaysia, Singapore, Japan, and finally, the long, long flight to New York, followed by a short flight to Chicago.

Today, there will be another Rotary Club make-up meeting on board ship. I used my walking tape each day, received evaluation for a fitness program by the spa director on board, and practiced my clarinet each day. There is a home talent show next week (Thanksgiving), but I think I'll not play.

## November 21, 2000

We arrived at the port of Oman around 10:00 a.m. today. This time, we did not take an organized tour but met up with a couple from Escondido, California, Kate and Paul, and shared a cab into the "souk" or marketplace. That turned out to be a big nothing: hot weather and bright sun but not much else. This country is exceedingly clean, few people speak English, and everyone seems to wear the galabayas (with pockets).

We took another cab into Salalah, the larger city in Oman, and wandered the streets, looking for a flag of the country. Al had gotten one in Djibouti, but we both forgot to get one in Egypt, even after we had four stops in that country. Al went into a bank in Oman, and not only did a nice young fellow take him directly to a shop to get the flag, but he would not allow Al to reimburse him for the cost. The flag was worth about $2.50US.

We took another cab back to the ship, cooled off, and changed clothes. We had lunch at the barbeque spot. I had a turkey burger with lots of hot sauerkraut and a glass of iced tea. Al had a slice of pizza and some tiny BBQ ribs. Then he went to the pier, and I went to our stateroom where I put the clarinet together, went out on our balcony, and posed for a picture with the clarinet, while Al stood on the dock and took the picture. Another passenger saw the clarinet and told him that there were three kinds of clarinets and that he used to play but thought his lips could not do it anymore.

Then I went into the spa and, following the program Mick the health director had worked out for me, I rode the bike for about ten minutes and got my heart rate up to 105rpm. Each day, I walk the fitness track with my walking tape or go on the bike in the spa. Yesterday I went into the saltwater pool and the Jacuzzi. It was very nice.

Last night, they had a new entertainer in the Cabaret Lounge. His name was Kier, and he played the guitar, harmonica, and piano, and did some comedy and some impressions. He was quite good.

For the past few days, the satellite hasn't worked, so we were unable to get BBC television in our rooms or send e-mails. Everyone was wondering about the election, but there was no way to get current news. At just about 3:00 p.m. today, the satellite was again working, but apparently, there were no election results. There was a mock election on board, and of course Bush won by about 3 percent of the votes. That did not surprise us, as the average person onboard appears to be an affluent Republican!

### November 23, 2000 - Thanksgiving aboard the R2

This is our second day on the Arabian Sea en route to Bombay (now Mumbai), our next port. We have been very busy loafing around the ship, playing Trivia (Al), exercising, eating, of course, meeting new people, and playing cribbage.

We signed up for three different tours, one in each of our next three ports. The trip has been fantastic. I bought a Seiko watch for $69.95 (a beauty), and I already had purchased an 18 carat bracelet for myself. I wanted to get gifts for Brian, Matt, Laura, Emily, and Ben and hoped to find something suitable at one of our next destinations.

## November 25, 2000

The traffic in Mumbai was incredibly crowded; people pack the streets, and barbershops are right on the curbs. The currency is the Indian Rupee and $1.00US = 46.7 INR. Weather is sunny with a high of 95F and a low of 69F. We took the Bombay of the Raj Tour, which left the ship at 12:30 p.m. We saw the famous Gateway of India, the arch built in 1911 to commemorate the visit of King George V. We drove along Marine Drive, which borders the Indian Ocean, and went through fashionable Malabar Hill to the Jain Temple. We were to visit the Prince of Wales Museum, but when we got there, they had just lost all electrical power, and we could not enter. We drove past the Mint, the Town Hall, and the gothic-style Victoria Railway Terminal.

## November 26, 2000

The full name of Goa is Mormugao. The weather was sunny with a high of 95F and a low if 68F. The Portuguese had settled this part of India in 1505. Its reputation is for its silks, spices, porcelain, and pearls. St. Francis Xavier had strong influences in this area. Goa is one of India's prime tourist locations with 65 miles of beautiful beaches. After we left Goa, we sailed a distance of 165 nautical miles to New Mangalore.

## November 27, 2000

Yesterday we were in Goa, India, and took the Highlights of Goa Tour. We were on a bus for about an hour, stopped to shop, and visited three Catholic churches. It was hot and humid but not bad, and this city in India, which was part of Portugal until 1967, was very interesting. There were many beggars, though, but the city was trying to develop a large tourist trade, and they promoted the fact that they had four or five five-star resorts and terrific beaches.

We had an adventure there. After Al left the Church of the Born Jesus where a large Catholic mass was in progress, he said he didn't feel good and would wait for the tour bus. Another man, Cullom Comely of Houston, Texas, said he had recovered from hip surgery recently and that he would wait too. I decided to stay with both of them. We waited about fifteen minutes and then walked to the corner but no bus. We sat in the sun for almost an hour. Cullom walked over to the second church but no sign of tourists. He checked the corner and around the corner but no bus. All we saw were vendors selling stuff, beggars, and Indian families returning from or going to mass. We finally saw the bus. Our guide was very angry with us for leaving the tour. It turned out that they had been looking for us everywhere.

Last night, after a terrific dinner in The Club restaurant (very elegant), we watched a new entertainer do a musical tribute to Doris Day (good songs), met another couple from Florida, and played cribbage. I watched the movie "Saving Grace," part of "The Full Monty," and part of "Out of Africa," not all at once but in bits and pieces.

Today, we went on another half-day tour of Mangalore City, India. We had a great guide whose name was Preetha, twenty-one years old and a graduate student in business administration. She took us to the Mangaladevi Temple, a Hindi temple where a priest was praying, and we saw the three gods in the Hindu religion: Brahma, Vishnu, and Shiva. Our guide told us to walk around the temple in a clockwise circle, ring the bell when we entered, and ring it when you left. We had to take our shoes off before entering.

We also visited the St. Aloysius Chapel, inspired by the Sistine Chapel in Rome. This nineteenth century church is famous for its outstanding biblical fresco painted in 1889 by an Italian Jesuit priest, Moscheni. Following that, we visited the Rosario Cathedral, the ancient church of the holy rosary. We saw nursery schools, grade schools, and high schools. The kids were all dressed in the uniforms of their particular school. There are many universities and colleges in Mangalore, and, in general, this is a well-to-do city with few beggars, and much cleaner than any other.

Mangalore is a beautiful coastal city, mentioned in the manuscripts of the great library at Alexandria, Egypt. It's on the west coast of India and is a port on the mouth of the Nitras River. Mangalore is in the state of Karnataka, and although a minor port, it handles 75 percent of India's coffee exports and the bulk of its cashew nuts.

We visited a cashew nut factory. Cashews are a big export in India. The cashew is the only seed that grows on the outside of the fruit. Like the coconut, there is nothing wasted on the cashew. From the outer shell to the very nut inside, everything is usable as an ingredient in paint to fodder for animals, finally ending up as the very high-calorie and delicious cashew nut.

Some other interesting facts about India: Advertising of the anti-odor shirts is on billboards, as well as the Yellow Pages. The *bindi* is the vermillion dot put between the eyes on the forehead. One can also place a *kum-kum* or jeweled dot on the forehead. The *beedi* is a cheap form of cigarette. It is like a tiny cigar only a few pieces of tobacco, hand-rolled in a leaf and tied with a thread. The leaf varies, but one used in particular comes from the Camel's Foot Tree (Baubinia).

Preetha said that the caste system is not prevalent in India anymore except when there is a marriage. Arranged marriages are still quite common, and the parents try to find a mate for their child within the same caste. When a girl marries, no matter how poor the family is, the wedding usually has a minimum of one hundred guests. The bride places a ring on her second toe and wears black beads, which her husband puts on at the ceremony. She paints vermillion through a part in her hair. She also paints the palms of her hands and the top of her feet with henna decorations. Widows wear white gowns and rarely re-marry.

We also stopped at a street lined with stores. I went into the Children's Corner store to buy something for Ben and ended up getting him a dhoti (a white suit consisting of a jacket and a pair of trousers), a typical Indian outfit, which I've seen on men. Al continued his quest for a flag of India but so far no luck.

Tomorrow we travel one hundred ninety-nine miles to Cochin to visit the fourth city on our India sojourn. Cochin has the oldest Jewish synagogue in India, and then three days at sea.

## November 28, 2000

Cochin, India (population 686,000), is our last stop in India. We took one of the commercial tours, Highlights of Cochin, and learned quite a bit about this area. Cochin is in the state of Kerala. Our tour was by small motorboat, which took us to Old Cochin. The first place we docked was in Mattancheny. It seems that Cochin was once visited by King Solomon and was Columbus's intended destination. They call the city the Queen of the Arabian Sea, and it is quite lovely. Jew Town is in Mattancheny, although the term is used in a descriptive, not a derogatory way.

It seems that Cochin offered refuge to Jews more than two thousand five hundred years ago. There were once thousands of Jewish settlers here, but their numbers have dwindled to fourteen or so, and all but three or four are in their seventies. They did not leave because of persecution but went to Israel when it became an independent country.

One of the oldest synagogues in the world is Patradeshi Synagogue in Jew Town. Built in 1568, the synagogue has brass columns, hanging lamps from Belgium, and porcelain tiles from China. This was one of the most interesting places we visited on our trip, and we took a lot of pictures—Hebrew writing, menorahs, star of David, and, in one case, on a wrought iron balcony, the star of David juxtaposed next to what looked like a swastika. We had to take our shoes off before entering the synagogue, not because it was a religious requirement, but because visitors' shoes would ruin the floor tiles. Each tile (blue on white) is differ-

*Al at the entrance to Jew Town*

ent from the one next to it. The gold altar was beautiful.

We also visited the Dutch palace, which the Portuguese had built in 1555. The wooden ceilings in the Coronation Hall that the Dutch had added gave the palace its name. The Portuguese founded the first European colony in Kochi in the sixteenth century, and we could still detect their influence.

We visited St. Francis Church (St. Francis of Assisi) where we saw the tombstone marking the original burial place of Vasco da Gama. His remains later went to Portugal.

Then we visited the site where Chinese fishermen were using unusual nets to catch the fish. We took pictures of this unfamiliar way of fishing. We returned by boat to the ship after spending time in the market places where I bought an outfit (cotton two-piece) for $5.00 (and they shortened the pants while I waited, for no charge). Al bought a white cotton shirt (Indian style) for himself and another one for either Sandy or one of the boys. I also bought a beautiful scarf, a necklace, two flutes, and an unusual gourd instrument. Our total spending was $20!

After returning to the ship, we were extremely sweaty as the temperature and humidity was in the 90s, so we showered and put on bathing suits and went on deck. We had been sitting in the hot sun on the top deck of the boat, so we were really glowing (at least I was). Al forgot to bring his cap, so he bought a beautiful straw hat for $1, and we bought a set of postcards with photographs of the synagogue, among others, including one showing how the cashew fruit grows.

We dressed in our new clothes and went to dinner in The Club restaurant, which featured an Indian menu (or an American one). We chose the Indian menu, and everything was delicious.

We ate with two other couples, and after introducing ourselves, we learned that one couple was from the Seattle area and the other, while born and raised in Detroit, currently had homes in Palm Springs, California, and Maui, Hawaii. Among their many businesses were restaurants in Hawaii and California. He was seventy-six, and she was a bit younger, but they met in junior high in Detroit, traveled all over the world, and just returned (prior to this voyage) from a trip that started in Bergen, Norway, and ended in North Cape, just south of the North Pole.

She is a gourmet cook, her husband said, and she gave me her recipe for Osso Bucco, among other things. They were very great people, and we have found that to be true with most of the people we encountered on the ship. They travel extensively, are mostly retired, and are quite well to do. I have met a forensic archaeologist; the owner of a day care center who lives full-time in Mazatlán, Mexico; doctors; lawyers; bankers; computer software developers; and more.

We took the Northern Island and Cultural Tour. We rode on an air-conditioned bus and visited a Thai Buddhist temple where a 108-foot-long statue of a reclining Buddha lies in a gigantic hall. We visited the Butterfly Farm and stopped at a batik factory where we watched how workers use waxes and dyes to create beautiful fabrics. Naturally, we bought a man's batik shirt for one of the boys.

After leaving Cochin, we traveled 1,470 nautical miles to Phuket, Thailand. The weather prediction was for a "chance of rain," but it didn't rain. Currency in Thailand is $1.00US = 43.8 Bahts.

### December 2, 2000 Phuket, Thailand

After three days at sea, we arrived in Phuket (pronounced "pooket"), Thailand. This time, we did not take a regular tour but rented a taxi with another couple from Muskegon, Michigan, and spent five and a half hours driving around this island. What a contrast to the other stops we have made! This island is clean, organized, and extremely beautiful. There are no beggars or street vendors chasing after you and pestering you. Nice shops, beautiful beaches and hotels. I wouldn't mind coming back and spending a week or two in Patang, one of the nicest-looking towns. We also stopped at a collection of Buddhist Temples and at a Thai Village where we saw a one-hour show featuring Thai music, dancers, kick boxing, sword/pole fighting, and some of the most beautiful costumes worn by the dancing girls.

When we were at the cultural show, I remarked to Al the amazing way the Thai dancers use their hands. I found out later that they train since early childhood to bend their hands backward, which gives their hands and fingers an incredible suppleness and range of motion; the hands dance as well as tell a story.

We also did some shopping. The money, called Bhat, is very unusual

*At a Buddhist temple*

looking, with a clear plastic space on the bills and of course a picture of their king.

Eloise and Dick Gillard, the other couple, were delightful to know.

She was an attorney, and they had been in the mortgage business for years. They had traveled everywhere, owned a home right on Lake Michigan with a private beach, and also three or four time-shares, one in Orlando, one on St. Maartens, and one other. Two companies were in the business of exchanging time-shares with other owners in other parts of the world. The Gillards had been to Banff, Switzerland, and other places under this arrangement.

### December 3, 2000 Penang, Malaysia
In Penang, Malaysia, the weather was 86F high and 77F low, and the currency, the Ringgitt, was $1.00US = 3.8 MR.

We stopped at the Penang Cultural Center where we saw a show of royal and folk dances from the different states in Malaysia. There was a demonstration of blowgun shooting, and I volunteered to blow one. I missed the target but it was fun. From Penang, we traveled 173 nautical miles to Port Klang, Malaysia.

### December 4, 2000 Port Klang, Malaysia
We signed up for a full-day tour called Kuala Lumpur Delights. We rode in an air-conditioned bus to the Sultan Salehuddin Mosque (blue dome mosque) which is the second largest in the world. We also stopped at one of the largest and most ornate Chinese temples in the area. We toured the Lake Gardens where they grow orchids and the national flower of Malaysia, the hibiscus. Next to the orchid garden is the Bird Park where thousands of birds fly freely in a totally natural environment.

### December 5, 2000 Malacca, Malaysia
On the way back to the ship in the tender, the driver hit every possible wave. I think he did it on purpose! Al, a few others, and I were completely soaked by the time we boarded. However, even though we were wet, the water was warm and very salty, and we had a good time laughing.

## December 6, 2000

These were the final days of our cruise. Monday we hit Port Klang, Malaysia, and visited Kuala Lumpur on a prepared tour. We had a terrific tour guide and drove from Port Klang all the way to Kuala Lumpur, a distance that took about an hour. On the way, we were impressed with the beautiful buildings and cleanliness of this country. Kuala Lumpur is famous for the Petronas twin towers that are supposed to be the tallest in the world. Our guide said that the Sears Tower was still taller by a small amount. We could not go into the towers, and I didn't even get a picture.

We made port in Malacca, Malaysia, and did not take a tour. There was not a port for the ship to dock, so it anchored outside of the area, and we took a tender into town. The tenders held one hundred and fifty as a lifeboat and one hundred and twenty as a traveling vehicle. They had windows in the front, and it was great racing with the waves across the Straits of Malacca to land.

When we arrived there, the usual cab drivers hawked their rides— tri-shaws, a kind of a two-seater, motorized rickshaw. Instead, we shared a cab with another passenger, David, by name. Al and David negotiated with a driver who said he had an air-conditioned car and spoke English. Well, the air conditioning was terrible, and we ended up with "240 air" (two windows open, forty miles per hour). He drove us around for about an hour, asking if we wanted to shop (no), visit various churches and temples (no) or see museums or galleries (no). Mostly, we looked around and stopped at four different shops, looking for hearing-aid batteries for Al.

The ship was to leave port around 6:00 p.m., but we learned that we would not leave until 12:30 a.m. There was dancing poolside with the Renaissance orchestra, followed by Alan Brooks on the piano, followed by "This 'n That," a contest led by Ken Seghers, the cruise director. Both of us entered, and while I lost each time, Al won another fanny bag. People stood in the center, and Ken would ask a question with two answers. If we believed one answer was correct, we would step to the right or the left. When he gave the correct answer, only those who were on the correct side would stay, and the rest would sit down. Example: If Miss Piggy and Yoda were in a fight, who would win? Miss Piggy or

Yoda? The answer, Miss Piggy. OR Who said "A rose by any other name would smell as sweet"? Was it Romeo or Juliet? The answer, Juliet.

## December 6, 2000 Singapore

We awoke to find ourselves in Singapore, a city-state. It is a country unto itself. We took a three-hour bus tour and learned quite a bit about the history of Singapore, how it became an independent country, and all about the various ethnic groups that had settled here. We visited India Town, China Town, Arab Town, and Malaysia Town, and saw where the Jewish immigrants settled. Singapore could set an example for the whole world. There are no beggars, slums or dirt. They have very strict laws. For example, one could be arrested for jaywalking, chewing gum, not flushing a public toilet, etc. (listed in a copy of the *Great Times Newsletter*), and they have special police, making sure that no one disobeys the law. Crime is virtually unknown, and walking anywhere, anytime is safe.

No tour, weather cloudy with a high of 86F and low of 76F. Currency: $1.00US = 1.75SD. We'd like to come back some day. This looks like one of the world's most interesting cities.

A large part of the city, built on landfill, is absolutely beautiful and modern. The architecture of the buildings is excellent, the shops and streets neat and clean, and the people friendly.

After the tour, we returned to the ship, had lunch, and went out again. It was very hot and humid, and while we were in one of the buildings, it rained for the first time on this trip. We've been so lucky with the weather—every day sunny and beautiful, and of course, as we are about forty miles north of the equator, the heat is intense.

We left our bags outside our cabin door by midnight. We had a continental breakfast in the Panorama buffet from 3:00 to 4:00 a.m. and then assembled in the Cabaret Lounge to disembark at 4:15 a.m. to catch a bus to the airport and then fly to Tokyo. After a two- to three-hour wait in Tokyo, we took a non-stop flight to JFK, New York, changed airports to LaGuardia, and flew to Midway, Chicago.

# New Challenges & Reflections

I have faced many challenges in my life, but the most recent one has really affected my future plans. It happened on November 30, 2015. I was still doing my radio show, *Getting to Know You*, and was interviewing Bill Jorgensen from the Del Fiore Jorgensen Funeral Home when, for some reason, I seemed to have a little trouble conducting the interview. I couldn't get my thoughts and questions out. I had to signal the recording engineer to stop recording a couple of times while I got myself together.

That evening, while watching TV, something happened, and I remember thinking, 'I ought to call somebody' because I felt I needed some help. I remembered that my youngest son, Marty, would be driving home from work. He lived nearby. I reached for the phone, which was on the table next to where I was sitting, but I found it hard to pick it up. I couldn't seem to grab it. When I finally did, it was upside down. I turned it around and then I thought, 'How do I use it? I have to push some buttons but how?' I guess I finally did it right because later Marty said I had dialed him four times. I don't remember much more, but suddenly Marty and my next door neighbor Patty were at my house. Patty said I should call 911 and go to the emergency room at a nearby hospital. I argued with her that I didn't need to go, but since she had been a nurse, I finally agreed.

The EMT took me in an ambulance to Sherman Hospital where I spent several days and learned that I had had a stroke! I was very lucky because while it left me with my left side feeling numb, I was able to walk and use my hands. I was functioning pretty normally, and I was telling people I had a TIA (transient ischemic attack). But Dr. Zamir said, "No, you had a stroke." I guess I'm pretty lucky not to have suffered any other problems. Dr. Zamir sent me to a neurologist who put me on some medications, advised me to stop driving, and cautioned me to "take it easy."

I put my auto insurance in storage until I could drive again. But after six months with no other "event" as the doctors call a stroke, I received the "all clear" to drive, and I started going on local errands again.

But the enormity of what had happened finally sank in, and I began thinking that perhaps I should sell my house and move into a retirement facility. I had heard about Clarendale, a new facility that was being built near me.

After having been with Al for so many years, I learned how to analyze things before making a decision. I began listing all of my current expenses that I wouldn't have in Clarendale, and it turned out to be around $1,500 a month. My new apartment will cost about $2,900 a month. So while almost doubling my expenses, I'm gaining security, and that's worth a lot. So, I put a small deposit down for a one-bedroom, one-bathroom apartment. My expected move-in date will be sometime in October.

My biggest physical problem is balance. It's gotten so bad that I walk with a walker almost everywhere. I worry that if I should fall, I may need help. In this new facility, help is available right outside my apartment door. Also there are all kinds of activities going on, plus trips and other things. I'll miss my large, beautiful home and my Sun City friends, but I know I'm doing the right thing.

I am lucky to have met my wonderful husband Al and to have shared sixty-plus years of a joyous marriage; to have my four terrific sons and my lovely daughters-in-law, Doris and Karin; my six grandchildren (in order of youngest first, Ben, Emily, Laura, Matt, Brian and Kendall); my nieces Nancy and Susan and nephew Norman; and great friends and all the activities that keep my mind engaged.

As I reflect on my ninety years, I have had a great life: terrific parents, grandparents, friends and co-workers. I've experienced interesting new adventures in work and play but also pain and loss. The love of my life was my wonderful Al and the four sons we had together. Our sons are smart, caring men, wonderful husbands and fathers. They are now beginning to take care of me, helping me with shopping, solving problems, and just being there.

People have asked if I have a secret for living. They say "curiosity killed the cat," but I have always been curious about how things work and still am to this day. I think that keeps my mind fresh and my spirit young. I love learning about everything—new technology, food, and cultures as well as history. I am fascinated with medical TV shows! I think I would have been very happy as a medical doctor. My kids call me "Dr. Mom."

I also really believe "you are what you eat." Also good genes and, of course, luck. Remember serendipity, which I define as "being in the right place at the right time." The dictionary definition might be different, but that's how I interpret the word.

Shakespeare sums up all life when he wrote in his famous poem:

> *All the world's a stage*
> *And all the men and women merely players.*
> *They have their exits and entrances*
> *And one man in his time plays many parts.*

As a player, I seem to have followed the script of the seven acts from the first "infant mewling and puking in his nurse's arms" to the "last scene of all," although I'm not quite ready for that!

I don't know about me "mewling and puking," but as the story goes, I was a colicky baby, crying and keeping my parents up all night. Now that I reached the seventh stage, I have no regrets or complaints. As I aged, I watched my physical body change. It started with a simple hammertoe in my eighties and graduating to balance issues, back problems, incontinence, restless sleep, loss of height, teeth loss, reduced eyesight, and the beginning of hearing problems, but it's OK.

My traveling days are really over, but I do hope I can make two more trips. I want to go to Iowa in May 2017 to attend my granddaughter Laura's graduation from pharmacy school. (Finally, a doctor in the family!) And I'd like to go to California the same month to attend my great niece's wedding and to see Doug's new home on the bay—his yacht. For now, I'm comfortably ensconced in my beautiful home, and as to the future…we'll see.

*My family at my ninetieth birthday party*